P9-CDP-457

4 vols

T_2

THE GREAT BOOKS:

A CHRISTIAN APPRAISAL

-v.1-
Ref.

Hutchins, R. M., ed.

THE
GREAT BOOKS

A CHRISTIAN APPRAISAL.

A Symposium on the First Year's Program
of the Great Books Foundation

Edited with an introduction
by Harold C. Gardiner, S.J.
Literary Editor of "America"

THE DEVIN-ADAIR COMPANY

NEW YORK

001
H974
.G25.G2
—v.1— Ref.

COPYRIGHT, 1949, BY

THE DEVIN-ADAIR COMPANY

---

*All rights reserved. Permission to
reproduce material from this book
must be obtained from the publishers.*

Third Printing

Printed in the United States of America

Foreword

LIBERAL education is education appropriate to man. It is education which holds before the rising generation the habitual vision of greatness. It is education concerned not with relative ends and the immediate adaptation of the individual to existing surroundings, but with values independent of time or particular environment.

The liberal course of study will therefore emphasize speech, conceptual thought, the capacity for tradition, aesthetic, intellectual, and spiritual experience and satisfaction. It will train the students in the arts of communication and give them a common stock of ideas and ideals. It will offer them models of greatness. It will attempt to help them learn to think, and to think about the most important questions, the aims and possibilities of human life and of organized society.

This means a curriculum composed of the great books, the great experiments, and the liberal arts, that is, language and mathematics. The great books are models of greatness. They raise the great issues. They display the aims and possibilities of human life and of organized society. They embody the tradition of the Western World. They have made us what we are. They suggest what we may be. They are, whether we know it or not, the cement which holds together such community as we have.

When some of the great masterpieces of the past are being read and studied from a pragmatic and even materialistic viewpoint, it is refreshing to find an appraisal of the Great Books and of their contribution to our civilization based on Christian concepts.

ROBERT M. HUTCHINS

University of Chicago
December 1948

Preface to the Revised Edition

THIS new edition of Volume I of the Great Books Series has been enlarged to include selections from the Bible, which have been newly added to all the Great Books courses. They are Chapters 11 and 12 from the Second Book of Samuel and Chapter 21 from the First Book of Kings, as found in the King James Version.

For comparison, the editor thought it advisable to include the corresponding passages in the Douay Version, these being found under the same chapter numbers in, respectively, II Kings and III Kings.

The differences in nomenclature between the Douay (Catholic) and King James (Protestant) versions of the Bible are explained in a note by J. Elliott Ross on page 109, taken from his discussion *Catholicism as Creed and Life,* which is in turn reprinted from *The Religions of Democracy* by Louis Finkelstein, J. Elliott Ross, and William Adams Brown, published by Devin-Adair.

Introduction

ANY MOVE to broaden the bases of popular culture is, without doubt, a movement in the direction of making truly democratic ideals more operative in American life. Though it cannot be maintained, and our Founding Fathers would never have maintained, that education alone is enough to assure an intelligent, interested and morally competent general public, it is nevertheless true that it is rather difficult to conceive such a general public if education, in a wide sense of the word, be lacking.

It follows, therefore, that contemporary interest in a study of the world's Great Books has within it the potentiality of broadening the bases of true democratic concepts and life by supplying one facet of education. Mr. Mortimer Adler, one of the directors of the Great Books Foundation, has singled out this aspect of a study of the Great Books, when he says: "The significance of the Great Books is their utility in universal adult education. Democracy cannot function successfully without a liberally educated electorate. . . . To achieve the kind of liberal education for which all schooling is, at best, a preparation, adults must make every effort to keep their minds active by engaging in self-education. . . . It is to serve them in this process that the Great Books perform their essential educational function. . . . They are concerned with the relatively few basic ideas, through the discussion of which men have gained insight, clarified their common problems and directed their thinking in every field of subject matter."

Insofar as the Great Books, therefore, can and will contribute to such a happy conclusion, familiarity with them, and the widening of that familiarity to include all American citizens capable of pursuing their study, is a matter for every citizen's concern and interest.

There are, however, several considerations that force themselves upon one who is asking this result from the Great Books. These considerations are by no means of such a nature as to negate the ideals looked for in a study of the Great Books, but I do think they have to be pondered rather carefully so that students of the Great Books do not either expect the impossible from them or engage in their discussion under misapprehension.

The first consideration is the very objective one: what makes a book great? I do not mean here to get into the endless controversies as to why such-and-such a book is included in a list of the Great Books and such-and-such a book is not. I suppose any separate lists of a hundred Great Books drawn up by eminent authorities would vary by thirty or forty per cent. I am rather interested in the idea that must be kept clearly before the student that a book may be great, though entirely wrong, and even vicious. A book will have been great if it has changed man's thinking, whether for good or evil, just as, if I may use the comparison, Hitler was undoubtedly a great man; one who changed the face of the world as he did is bound to be historically immortal, though ignominious.

Hence, the student should not approach a study of the Great Books with the notion that he is going to find in them only the great, noble, uplifting thoughts that men have conceived. It may be regrettable that such thoughts are not the only ones to be found in books that have moved or shaped our world and its civilization, but, though regrettable, it is a fact, and a study of the Great Books has to be, first and foremost, a study of human thought as it has existed, and not as it might have been better for it to exist. After all, the study of the Great Books is simply a study of human nature, and it is human nature, both at its best and at its worst, which is the proper study of man.

The second consideration has to do with the expectations one can legitimately entertain in approaching the Great Books. What are these books supposed to tell you? They are supposed to be a clarification of some of the basic problems that have always puzzled or exercised the human mind—duty, law, the good, the beautiful, justice and its source, the relationship of individual to individual and of society to the individual, etc. It would be unfair to expect any one of the Great Books to answer any of these questions with absolute clarity, certitude and finality. What we do have the right to expect is to find great minds illuminating the problems, casting them into clearer relief, shedding a glow on some of the obscurities, or else, by contrast, revealing the sad consequences when these truths are muffed or distorted. Indeed (and this aside is justified by the subtitle of this volume), all the Great Books, including those based on great Christian thinking, are a constant reminder of man's need of divine revelation for firm certitude on many truths that profoundly affect his earthly life and his eternal destiny. This point you will find underscored very neatly in Professor Schwarz' essay on Aristotle's *Politics.*

We have a right, then, to expect that each of the Great Books will play its peculiar part (either directly or indirectly) in our mental broadening, in our education. But what is the ultimate goal of such broadening? Here I must touch upon what I consider a grave inadequacy in the philosophy of education which lay behind the Great Books Foundation at its inception. This philosophy was incorporated largely in a *Handbook for Discussion Leaders,* published by the Foundation and prepared by Mortimer J. Adler. I understand that the handbook has now been abandoned and withdrawn from circulation and, in commenting upon it, I may, to some extent, be knocking over a straw man. But I think the point is well worth making in any Christian evaluation of the Great Books. The point is this. If discussion of the Great Books can well be a splendid tool for adult liberal education, then we must have fairly clear ideas on what a liberal education is. The happily suppressed handbook was very clear in its ideas on liberal education but, I think, inadequate. According to that original philosophy, a liberal education is one which educates man *as* man. Accordingly, the argument ran, liberal education has nothing to do with man as an animal (the whole field of physical education), nor anything to do with man as a spiritual being (the whole field of religious education). The inadequacy here lies in the simple fact that man, as man, is precisely a rational animal. Man is not being educated as a man if his physical education is entirely neglected and, above all, he is not being educated as man if his intellect and will are not being developed under education to the crown of their activity, which is knowledge and love of God. Notice I am not saying here anything about supernatural knowledge; revelation is another matter, but the mere human exercise of mind and will is being stunted if their exercise in knowledge and love of God is denied.

Indeed, many of the Great Books to be discussed in this volume and succeeding ones are books which deal precisely with God. In this volume, St. Augustine's *Confessions,* St. Thomas' *Treatise on Law,* come to mind as examples. If, then, discussion on these books will ultimately lead to a discussion of man's relation to God, then, in the discussion the participants are being educated to a knowledge of God and the very technique of the discussion will almost inevitably deny the inadequate philosophical assumption of such a truncated "liberal" education. Again, note that I am not saying that participants in a discussion that dwells upon man's relation to God will necessarily put their discussion into practice. That is another point. But they will be learning about man's relation to God and insofar they will be being educated as spiritual beings.

Let's pass on now from these considerations, which I mean to be suggestive rather than definitive, on the intrinsic nature of the Great Books, to some remarks on the discussion technique which the Great Books Foundation rightly emphasizes as one of the attractive and important aspects of the study. Since the Great Books discussions are designed almost exclusively for adult participation, it is a simple matter of practical necessity that their study be conducted in discussion form. Adults do not like to go back to school, in the sense of simply being lectured to, and furthermore it is true that it is a democratic process to arrive at some conclusions by a free interchange of ideas. It is not only a matter of practical necessity; it's a matter of pedagogical acuteness, because conclusions which have not been rammed down one's throat but arrived at sincerely in the give-and-take of discussion are most likely conclusions that will make the deepest and most lasting impression.

However, in this pedagogical method there are obvious booby-traps. First, if a discussion is to be fruitful it must actually arrive somewhere. If discussants of the Great Books go home after a two-hour session on St. Augustine's *Confessions* and have been able to reduce their discussion to no statements of a conclusive nature, then they will have done nothing but exercise themselves in a bit of mental and verbal gymnastics. This is where the leader of a discussion group finds his precise role. The ideal leader is one who will be able to draw out conclusions, not by imposing his own ideas, but by adroitly bringing out and balancing the ideas of members of his group and by having them show one another that the ideas they hold may have to be modified, readjusted, re-aligned. And here, of course, is where we run into another difficulty with some of the initial educational philosophy of the Great Books Foundation. To the Foundation, the idea of "teaching" is abhorrent because the conception they entertain is that all teaching is, of its nature, dogmatic. As a matter of fact, this guidance which discussion leaders simply have to give, if they are to fulfil their function, *is* a kind of teaching, and hence the importance, from a Christian viewpoint, of having discussion leaders who have themselves evaluated the Great Books Christian-wise and who know how to lead their groups to evaluate the books from a like viewpoint.

The purpose of this series of essays on the Great Books and of the subsequent volumes in the series is precisely to give some aid in these two difficulties. First of all, I do not think it advisable or even possible for discussants of the Great Books to enter a session with no ideas of their own. They are supposed naturally to have read the book before they discuss it, and, by the very fact of reading, if they have read at all intelligently, they are bound to have some ideas about the book. Hence, I feel it is but common sense that they enter the discussion with at least sound minimum ideas. The very least of a minimum is that they should know what the Great Book is actually about—the gist, the core of it—so that they may begin the discussion with the nucleus and then be able to branch out from this solid basis. I have too often experienced discussion groups arriving at a consideration of what a book is really about only after several hours of beating around the bush. This is by no means to hold the big stick over the student and tell him that he must think so-and-so about the subject matter of the book, but it is to put the subject matter clearly before him so that he and the discussion leader and others in the group may then go on to say, "Here is what the book says. Now, what do we think about it?" And secondly, "Now, what do we think about it as Christians?"

It is my sincere hope that this series of studies will help future participants in discussion to arrive more expeditiously and fruitfully at the education and widening of culture (in a full sense of the word) and hence at a finer citizenship, to which the Great Books can give no inconsiderable impetus.

I must now touch upon a matter which will be of concern only to Catholic participants in the Great Books discussions. In each year's group of books there are one or more which will be found on the *Index Librorum Prohibitorum*. This is not the place to discuss the *Index* of prohibited books, but I am in duty bound to point out to Catholics that under the law they are not allowed, without proper permission, to read these books. This is a problem which must be solved by each Catholic in his particular setup. It may be that some dioceses will give a general permission; it may be that in other dioceses the permission will have to be sought for each individual book. This, as I say, may vary from place to place. Among the books discussed in this volume, for example, two, those by Rousseau and Montaigne, are prohibited books. Non-Catholics who may read these words will, I hope, not take them as an occasion to raise the exaggerated cry that Catholic freedom of inquiry and independence of thought is tyranically regimented by the existence of the *Index*.

Someone has said that the only advantage to be gained from such discussions of the Great Books is that they produce Great Bookworms. This, unfortunately, may be true, if the whole program is not based on some sound principles, a few of which I hope these remarks have succeeded in pointing out. A final sound principle is this. Our approach to the Great Books should be one of intellectual modesty. I do not mean that some of the Great Books cannot be and do not have to be criticized severely from a Christian viewpoint. But not one of the books, even those with which we may disagree heartily, should be approached or judged in a spirit of intellectual arrogance. And after they have been approached and sampled and judged, the attitude of mind must still be one of intellectual humility. It would be a sorry result of all the Great Books discussions if participants came away thinking that because they had sampled a St. Thomas they therefore were experts on him. One result of Great Books discussions which can make for a better American citizen is if the discussions foster in the student a spirit of temperate judgment, a spirit of avoidance of extremes, a spirit of realization that even the greatest achievements of the human mind are always and inevitably reminders of human frailty and inadequacy.

True democracy can never be arrogant because true democracy, not mere political democracy, is a brotherhood of man, and a brotherhood of man is only possible because God is our Father.

HAROLD C. GARDINER.

Contents

Foreword . . . . Robert M. Hutchins   v

Introduction . . . . . . Harold C. Gardiner   vii

The Declaration of Independence
                   Robert C. Hartnett   1

PLATO: *Apology, Crito, Gorgias* . Edwin A. Quain   8

THUCYDIDES: *History* . . . . Edwin A. Quain   14

ARISTOPHANES: *Lysistrata, Birds, Clouds*
                   Edwin A. Quain   19

ARISTOTLE: *Ethics, Book I* . . . .
             Dietrich von Hildebrand   25

ARISTOTLE: *Politics, Book I* . Balduin V. Schwarz   28

PLUTARCH: *Lycurgus, Numa* and *Comparison,*
     Alexander and *Caesar* . . . Edwin A. Quain   33

ST. AUGUSTINE: *Confessions, Books I–VIII*
                   Frank Sheed   39

ST. THOMAS: *Treatise on Law* . Walter Farrell   44

MACHIAVELLI: *The Prince* . . John K. Ryan   50

MONTAIGNE: *Selected Essays* . . . Jean Misrahi   61

SHAKESPEARE: *Hamlet* . . . William J. Grace   70

LOCKE: *Of Civil Government*
                   Robert C. Hartnett   78

ROUSSEAU: *The Social Contract*

Louis J. A. Mercier   85

Federalist Papers .   .   .   . Robert C. Hartnett   92

ADAM SMITH: *The Wealth of Nations*

George G. Higgins   98

KARL MARX: *Communist Manifesto*

Nicholas S. Timasheff   104

THE BIBLE: *Selections*   109

Notes on the Contributors   124

THE GREAT BOOKS:

A CHRISTIAN APPRAISAL

The Declaration of Independence

THE GREAT books program, the subject of this series of volumes, very ingeniously provides for an opening "sample" discussion on the first two sentences of The Declaration of Independence. This document was chosen, no doubt, because of its intrinsic "meatiness" and great contemporary importance. It has the merit of being brief and familiar. But it has the further merit of illustrating how classical writing is packed with thought. It would, indeed, be a great mistake to imagine that it can be used to school a group in the mere technique of discussing a piece of writing. For The Declaration, if seriously analyzed, will carry a discussion-group into the deepest waters of political philosophy.

The opening paragraph of this great document takes the high ground of asserting that the American people are ready "to assume among the Powers of the earth, the equal station to which the Laws of Nature and of Nature's God entitle them." Then follows the majestic declaration:

> We hold these truths to be self-evident, that all men are created equal, that they are endowed by their Creator with certain unalienable Rights, that among these are Life, Liberty and the pursuit of Happiness. That to secure these rights, Governments are instituted among Men, deriving their just powers from the consent of the governed, That whenever any Form of Government becomes destructive of these ends, it is the Right of the People to alter or abolish it, and to institute new Government, laying its foundations on such principles and organizing its powers in such form, as to them shall seem most likely to effect their Safety and Happiness.

In this resume of traditional Western political philosophy we have summed up the natural equality of all men, their possession of natural rights, the moral purpose and origin of the State and the right of revolution, if necessary, to achieve that purpose.

The first paragraph lodges the colonists' case for independence on their rights under "the Laws of Nature and of Nature's God."

Now the concept of "natural law" plunges the reader straight into the heart of ethics. We are dealing with a highly philosophical idea.

What is the scope of philosophy? How can one perceive metaphysical reality? What is the difference between the philosophical and, let us say, the scientific method of inquiry used in the natural sciences? What is the difference between a *truth* and a *fact?* Fortunately, St. Thomas studies the idea of natural law from a purely philosophical point of view in another great book included in the first year's program of reading and discussion, his classic *Treatise on Law.* But the student of The Declaration must remember that he has not yet analyzed this work of St. Thomas, and he will find when he does that it is no mental "pushover."

But another difficulty emerges. Different writers have used the same term, "natural law," to designate quite opposite views. Long before St. Thomas, the Stoics used the term. Cicero used it freely. What did they mean by it? If a student consults Charles H. Ilwain's *The Growth of Political Thought in the West,* he will find that Roman jurists like Gaius and Ulpian took opposite sides on the exact meaning of the "natural law." The one identified it with the laws governing the universe as a whole, and thought that it applied to "beasts and birds" as well as to men. The other thought that it was specifically a *human* law, a law governing rational and free creatures. In what sense did the signers of The Declaration use the term? One of them, James Wilson, wrote a long essay on the subject.

Louis M. Hacker in his recent two-volume work, *The Shaping of the American Tradition,* voices a common-enough view when he says:

> Ours is a government of laws and not of men. Highest of all is the natural law which Jefferson, obtaining the notion from John Locke, embodied in the Declaration of Independence. [Vol. I, p. xxi].

If Jefferson obtained the notion of natural law from John Locke, then we are thrown back into the inquiry as to what Locke's "notion" of natural law was. It so happens that Locke's second treatise, *Of Civil Government,* also appears on the list of Great Books to be read and discussed during the first year of the program. Are we therefore going to defer our analysis of what "the Laws of Nature and Nature's God" mean in The Declaration until we study John Locke? That might well be the best thing to do. But when that time comes it will be well to recall that Carl Becker in his *The Declaration of Independence* goes to great lengths in order to show that the signers of The Declaration did *not* get their idea of natural law from John Locke at all. And Jefferson, who drafted The Declaration, wrote in a letter that the "sentiments" incorporated in the document were "those of all America." He mentioned several authors as contributing to the "shaping of the American mind," including Locke; but he seemed to put more stress on the general currency of the ideas. Locke's concept of natural law, which is analyzed in a later chapter, is actually far too individualistic to rhyme with the thinking of the signers of the Declaration.

One could do worse than to dip into the late Dr. James J. Walsh's *The Education of the Founding Fathers* to find out where the educated leaders of that generation of Americans did get their concept of natural law. Certainly Jean Jacques Burlamaqui cannot be left out of account. Have you ever heard of him? Did you know that his *The Principles of Natural and Politic Law* was a widely disseminated, widely read and highly respected treatise at the time of the drafting of The Declaration? His understanding of the moral law governing human nature is quite in accord with Thomistic philosophy.

The purpose of the Great Books courses is to open up the minds of readers by bringing them into immediate contact with writings of permanent value. In the case of the writing chosen as a "sample," it becomes clear at the start that this is no simple operation. In fact, very few Americans will find that they are equipped to lead the discussion on the first paragraph with ease.

Every phrase in the second paragraph presents a challenge. But let us pass over the question of "self-evident" truths (even "truths" would bear a good deal of analysis), of being "created equal," and of "unalienable rights." The definition of these rights is what intrigues us.

The rights singled out as of transcendent significance are of those of "Life, Liberty, and the pursuit of Happiness." This phrase looks simple enough. But is it?

First let us compare this statement with that in the famous Bill of Rights of the first Constitution of the State of Virginia, the work of George Mason, with the help of Madison and, to a lesser extent, of Jefferson. Article I reads as follows:

Section 1. Equality and rights of men. That all men are by nature equally free and independent and have certain inherent rights, of which, when they enter into a state of society, they cannot, by any compact, deprive or divest their posterity, namely, the enjoyment of life and liberty, with the means of acquiring and possessing property, and pursuing and obtaining happiness and safety.

Do you notice any significant difference between the wording of this statement and that of The Declaration?

The Virginia Bill of Rights emphasizes the idea that "all men are by nature" (God as Creator is not mentioned) "equally free and independent." The Declaration carries no such phrase as "free and independent." Is the omission significant? Jefferson originally had the word "independent" in his early draft of The Declaration, but it is crossed out, as you can see for yourself in *The Complete Writings of Thomas Jefferson,* a very useful one-volume compilation edited by Samuel K. Padover. Does the inclusion or exclusion of the phrase really make any difference? Do you think that its inclusion gives the Virginia Bill of Rights a more *individualistic* ring than The Declaration? The slave-holders are said to have objected to it, but they had just as much reason for objecting to "created equal" and endowed with the right to "liberty" phrases they accepted.

But let us go on. The Virginia statement then lists the "inherent rights" which men bring into "a state of society" as "the enjoyment of life and liberty, with the means of acquiring and possessing property. . . ." Nothing is said in The Declaration about property. If you want to see something interesting, read Locke's second *Treatise of Civil Government,* with all he has to say about "the state of nature," "equality" and "property," and *then* ask yourself whether the Virginia Bill of Rights is not definitely Lockian in ways in which The Declaration is not.

If you want another example of a State constitution you might look up that of Massachusetts, adopted in 1780. It also opens with a "Declaration of Rights":

All men are born free and equal, and have certain natural, essential, and unalienable rights; among which may be reckoned the right of enjoying and defending their lives and liberties; that of acquiring, possessing, and protecting property; in fine, that of seeking and obtaining their safety and happiness.

This statement departs further from The Declaration in using the word "born." Has "born" the same connotation as "created"? Has a human person no rights until he is born into this world? This question has assumed considerable pertinence. It is not merely a question of destroying unborn life. It is a question of what society owes in the way of prenatal care to offspring which have not yet seen the light of day. And we usually associate with "birth" the whole complex of "accidents" by which, in the concrete, men are actually unequal in the human conditions and temporal circumstances of their lives.

Much has been written about human "equality." But, in the end, is not equality a moral concept? Is it not derived immediately from the fact that every human person is created by God as His human creature for the same sublime end, God Himself, for which all men are created? Is it a good idea to obscure this only ground of human equality by changing the clear affirmation of The Declaration that "all men are created equal" into the weaker and even ambiguous phrase, "born free and equal"? And is not a person normally "born" a member of society on which he is dependent rather than being completely free? Is not this so-called "sociality" of human nature at least as important as his right to be "free" from arbitrary and unjust interference? It does not seem whimsical to ask whether in the Massachusetts Bill of Rights, as in that of Virginia, more of Lockian individualism was allowed to find expression than in The Declaration of Independence.

The question cannot be answered with much satisfaction apart from a close reading of Locke himself. His second *Treatise of Civil Government* is an interesting if somewhat deceptive and inconsistent piece of writing. What one has to watch in it are the implications rather than the straightforward assertions. But if a person comes to it after having analyzed St. Thomas' *Treatise on Law*, the reading of which *is* a real intellectual challenge, he can begin to see a gulf widening between the two thinkers. The issues come into focus. Only then can he turn back to The Declaration to ask himself whether the political philosophy it embodies has a closer affinity to that of John Locke or that of St. Thomas.

For it seems very unlikely that political thinkers of the caliber of John Adams, Charles Carroll, John Witherspoon, and espe-

cially James Wilson, should have signed The Declaration if they
thought that it smacked of Lockian individualism. Wilson was
the most acute political philosopher of his generation, the only
one, indeed, who wrote at full length on such concepts as natural
law and the social nature of man in a scholastic sense. That he
was critical of Locke is perfectly plain from the way in which
he attacks Locke's theory of knowledge in his lecture, "On Man
as an Individual."

Those who embark upon the exhilarating experience of a great-
books reading program cannot expect to capture the sense of
great writings in one session devoted to each. What they learn
will depend in part on their previous academic training. It will
depend in part on their natural aptitude for the handling of somewhat elusive types of thinking. And it will depend in no small
part on the way in which the discussion leader directs the course
of the discussion, on the way he unfolds his questions, and on the
amount of time he allocates to various phases of the work under
consideration.

The ultimate question is this: what is the final purpose of such
a course of reading? If it is merely to encourage intellectual activity by confronting readers with a variety of lines of thinking,
will the groups move toward any integrated system of thought?
And if they do not move in that direction, is such intellectual
activity what they need and want? Academic detachment is good
in its place and to a proper degree. But the world is faced with
a mental confusion out of which only people with a coherent and
valid outlook can lead it. To expect the average reader to do his
own integrating is expecting a lot. Perhaps the guidance offered
in these chapters will help readers to move toward an integration
in their study of the Great Books.

But no purely human document is more worth the intellectual
effort required to plumb its meaning than our Declaration of
Independence. No other writing embodies in one smooth, eco-
nomical statement the values for which Western civilization today
stands ready to pour out its natural and, if need be, human re-
sources when faced with the challenge of those who would strip
mankind of its dignity and freedom in exchange for chimerical
promises of material prosperity. Other nations have constitutions
which imply, as does our own, a political philosophy. Only we
have an explicit statement of that philosophy in an official and

separate declaration, and ours traces its origin deep into the Christian tradition of which we are now the responsible heirs.

ROBERT C. HARTNETT

SELECTED BIBLIOGRAPHY

BECKER, Carl, *The Declaration of Independence.* Knopf.
BOYD, Julian, *The Declaration of Independence: The Evolution of the Text.* Washington: Library of Congress.
CHINARD, Gilbert, *Thomas Jefferson: The Apostle of Americanism.* Little, Brown.
JEFFERSON, Thomas, *The Writings of Thomas Jefferson* (ed. A. A. Lipscomb and A. E. Bergh), 20 vols. Washington: The Thomas Jefferson Memorial Association, 1903-05. See Index under "Declaration of Independence."
PADOVER, Saul K., *The Complete Jefferson.* Duell, Sloane and Pearce.

Plato: Apology, Crito, Gorgias

THE DAY before Socrates died in the municipal prison of Athens he spent the morning discussing with his old friend Crito the reasons why he had lived the life that he had and why he would on the following day drink the hemlock at the command of the magistrates of the State. The day of his death was passed in an elaborate debate on the immortality of the soul; when he died, his friends were sure that there had passed from their midst "the best, the wisest and the noblest man of our times." All through his life he had been dedicated to the pursuit of justice and he maintained a standard of morality that was as far superior to the traditional code of Homeric ethics as that was above the current teaching of his contemporaries, the Sophists.

In spite of all that, the official court of the State had condemned Socrates to death as an atheist and as a corrupter of the youth of the land. His friends had been unable to swing the vote in his favor at the trial or to extricate him before his execution and so, with a view to justifying the memory of his revered master, Plato told the heroic story in the three works mentioned here grouped together as a "great book"—*Apology, Crito* and *Gorgias*. If read together, they present us with a picture of the trial as a mockery of justice, showing clearly that Socrates refused every subterfuge out of conscious principle. The first two make it clear that Socrates practiced what he preached, for the Gorgias (ante-dated by Plato to 416 B.C.) is merely the theoretical statement of the principles on which he lived and died. All three tell the same story: Socrates believed (and died for his belief) that it was never honorable to do wrong or to requite injustice with injustice. Devotion to duty and an abstract ideal of virtue enshrines the noblest concept of morality human reason had thus far contrived.

The trial of Socrates took place in the Spring of 399 B.C. when he was accused by three of his enemies: of not believing in the gods sanctioned by the State, of introducing new gods and of being a corrupter of the youth. The judges were 501 citizens of Athens. Socrates all but refused to take his accusers seriously and what defense he offers is in the nature of an analysis of the prejudice that had grown up against him in the preceding twenty-five years, since he had been lampooned in *The Clouds* of Aristophanes. There he was portrayed as an irresponsible dreamer who pretended to esoteric knowledge "of things in the clouds and under the earth." The majority of his judges had grown up with the idea that Socrates was a fool and such is the power of ingrained prejudice that he has little hope of dispelling the effect of the slander. In fact, he does not try and merely offers a flat denial to the "charges" contained in the comedy of Aristophanes.

There is little reason to believe that the charge of atheism was ever seriously intended. There was at the time in Athens no concept of official religious orthodoxy and it is unlikely that any educated man of the time believed in the traditional mythology as a system of theology. His accuser, Meletus, had never clearly formulated the alleged crime in his own mind, if we are to judge from the ease with which Socrates, in his cross-examination, leads him into the blatant contradiction of asserting that Socrates believed in spiritual beings (his personal *daimon* which warned him whenever he was about to do wrong), and, in the next breath, that Socrates was a complete atheist.

The real grievance, the important reason for the hatred that inspired the arraignment was that Socrates was "a corrupter of the youth." It had been for many years the practice of Socrates to go about the streets of Athens, engaging in conversation with all who had a reputation for knowledge and wisdom. His normal procedure was to fasten on someone and question him about the reality and nature of virtue and goodness in general. Prominent politicians, noted poets and competent artisans, all had pat and ready answers to the questions, which Socrates, with a mild and disarming skepticism, proceeded to demolish, much to the discomfiture of his victims. Many years before, the oracle at Delphi, the central shrine of Greece, had stated that there was no man wiser than Socrates. This he felt hard to believe since he considered himself to be ignorant and it was in quest of someone wiser than himself that he tackled the pundits of his time. As a device for losing friends and alienating people, the method could hardly be bettered. He finally concluded that the god must mean that human knowledge is as nothing when compared to divine wisdom and thus a man is only wise when he knows that he does not know.

Quite naturally, such performances were vastly entertaining to the bright young men of Athens who flocked around Socrates and, what was worse for him, proceeded to imitate him. Hence he was supposed to be destroying the respect of the young for their reputable elders and this is the real reason why he had to be removed. We know from other works of Plato that Socrates held no very high opinion of politicians and it is quite likely that an exaggeration of his teachings could very well have engendered anti-democratic sentiments which had brought revolution and anarchy to Athens. Two of his closest friends among the young men, Alcibiades and Critias, were at the time considered to have been traitors to the State.

His only defense against the charge of corruption was that he had acted in this manner at the command of the god and he briefly alludes to the fact that the families of the young men had offered no condemnation of his influence in the past. His, he claimed, was a life of unselfish dedication and obedience to the command of the god. Far from being an enemy of Athens, he was really the divinely-appointed "gadfly" chosen to stir the Athenians from their lethargy and to turn their minds from the pursuit of wealth and honor to the true realities and the practice of virtue. Hence he protested he had done no wrong; rather than be condemned to death for his conduct, he should be supported at the expense of the State, since no one was more valuable to Athens than Socrates.

However, the laws, in the person of the Court, have decreed that he must die and, consistently with the principles of his life, he must obey their command. He refuses to influence the vote of the judges by playing on their feelings and assures them that he does not fear death. If he did, he would be pretending to know for certain something that he did not know. Death is either "a sleep and a forgetting," and hence has no terrors for him, or else, and it is to this view that he clearly inclines, it is merely the beginning of an immortal existence in which he will live with all the great figures of the past. Death is therefore no evil and he does no wrong in avoiding it; it is rather they who condemn him who do wrong. In the race of life, death runs faster but evil is harder to avoid.

Near the end of his imprisonment, Crito tries to persuade Socrates to escape and go into exile. He reminds him of his bereaved wife and children and tells him that he is taking the easier way, free of all responsibility. Once again Socrates returns to his principles. Since the laws have decreed that he must die, die he must in obedience to their command. Exile would be no escape since without hypocrisy he could not continue to teach his doctrine, were he to play false to his duty as a citizen and in cowardly fashion save his body, but bring ruin to his soul. No matter what the provocation, a man must live up to his agreements and obligations. Even though it means his death, Socrates will not despise the laws and thus do harm to the State and to his fellow-citizens.

In the *Gorgias* Plato tells the story of a meeting with the famous rhetorician which at first sight might seem to be wholly concerned with Rhetoric as an art, or, as Gorgias maintains, the queen of all the arts. But a closer examination will betray the fact that we have here a series of three questions which bring us from the character of the art of rhetoric to the sharply-divided ethical convictions involved in an estimate of that art and finally to the real point of the dialog—life and the way it should be lived. Socrates maintains that the life of devotion to the higher good is vastly superior to the theory and practice of the strong men who aim only at power, the domination of their fellow men, and the greatest injustice most handsomely done with complete impunity.

Gorgias holds that man's greatest good is freedom—the ability to do whatever he may please without hindrance; since rhetoric is the best means of getting what you want, rhetoric is the greatest of all arts. In his usual roundabout manner, Socrates forces his interlocutor to admit that rhetoric is nothing but a device whereby an ignorant man persuades an audience equally ignorant that he understands some things better than an expert.

Polus, however, is bolder than Gorgias and is willing to push his principles to their ultimate conclusions; he maintains that the happiest man is the one who can kill or imprison anyone and if rhetoric can help to that, so much the better. To this Socrates replies with his well-known view that to harm another is never good and the guilty man is better off when he has been punished since, as he deserves it, it is done justly, and hence, he has been treated with justice and has been improved. Conversely the man who sins with impunity is worse off than if he had been justly punished for his sins.

Callicles, the last speaker, is even more consistent than Polus. For him, it is only the weakling who will "put up" with injustice; the really strong men are aggressive and ruthlessly seek to gratify, at any cost, their own desires and impulses. This to Socrates is but legalized banditry and the men who act thus while ruling are supremely vicious. The true statesman is the man who sets for himself an ideal of temperance and justice and seeks to produce these in the souls of his subjects. The finest adornment of the statesman is the possession of moral values and his greatest talent is to be able to get the citizens to desire what is really good. When Callicles recommends that Socrates should go into politics, he is told that Socrates is the only real statesman in Athens for he is the only man who aims to do good to those with whom he speaks.

So firmly is Socrates convinced of the truth of this view that he protests that, if he should ever be brought to trial for his conduct, he would die rather than defend himself by unworthy means, or by doing any wrong. He would not fear death because the dreadful thing is not to die, but to go to the other world with a heavy burden of guilt. Then he tells the story that formerly men used to be judged while still alive but their true selves were not known because of the fair covering of the body. To prevent such mistakes, man is now judged after death, when his judges may see his naked soul. Then the incurably wicked will be eternally punished; such as are thought to be curable will pass through a period of purification; but when the judges find one who has lived a pure and holy life, him will they send to dwell forever in the Isles of the Blest.

Hence the advice that Socrates would give to Callicles is that the only good life is the life of goodness and holiness. It is better to suffer unjustly than to injure any man; a man should seek not so much to seem to be good as really to be good and noble both in private and in public; that rhetoric and every other art in life should be used for pointing to what is just. "Take my advice and follow my example and thus you will be happy in this life and in the life to come; in a word, live and die in the practice of justice and every other virtue."

The unity and coherence of these three works will thus be clear. Any discussion of them must stress the complete sincerity of Socrates and his adherence to his principles. Since in a sense Socrates "laid down his life for his friends," the motive of duty to the laws must be compared with the Christian motive of love. And the absence in Platonic morality of the ideals of Christian purity and meekness, out of love of Christ, should clearly be noted. The basic concepts involved in the structure of morality—death, immortality, duty, the sanctity of law, evil and its inevitable retribution—these are the contents of the gospel according to Socrates.

EDWIN A. QUAIN

SELECTED BIBLIOGRAPHY

GUARDINI, Romano, *The Death of Socrates.* Sheed & Ward.
BURNET, John, *Platonism.* University of California.
TAYLOR, A. E., *Plato, the Man and His Work.* Dial Press.
PLATO, *Dialogues.* Dutton (Everyman's Library).

Thucydides: History of the Peloponnesian War

No MOVEMENT in the history of Greece ever stirred the world as did the Peloponnesian War, the struggle between Athens and Sparta for the leadership of the Aegean world. For twenty-seven years at the close of the fifth century, B.C., these two Powers sustained the climax of the rivalry that had existed since they had both risen above the welter of independent City States which composed the political structure of the ancient world. Thucydides, an Athenian, wrote its history, since he realized from its beginning that this war was to be a greater event than any that had taken place in all former ages.

Nine chapters of this masterly work have been chosen as a "Great Book," and the selections, while a minuscule part of the whole, do touch upon the essential features of the work and the story of the war. The first is a portion of "The Archaeology," wherein Thucydides looks into the remote past to set the stage for the conflict and to adumbrate the key principles of his history. The second is the incident at Plataea which caused the outbreak of the war in 431. The third tells of the situation at Sparta that led to the abortive Peace of Nicias in 421, the turning point of the dramatic structure of the whole work. This is followed by the speech of Alcibiades which persuaded Athens to embark on the disastrous Sicilian Expedition in 416, and the last is a detail of the Revolt of the Allies in 412 that marked the downfall of the Athenian empire. The brevity of the selections suggests that they are intended merely to point the way to a more extended reading of the history. Therefore the following remarks will tend to clarify their contexts and to link them together into an orderly picture of the high points of the progress of the war.

Out of the struggle of the Persian wars, which ended with Thermopylae and Salamis and broke the domination of the Barbarian over the Hellenic world, Athens arose as the only naval power of the times. To consolidate the gains of freedom from the Persians, there was formed a voluntary confederacy of Delos in 478. The members, besides Athens, were the City States on the west coast of Asia Minor, the Aegean Sea and the eastern shores of Greece. Graduated tributes were to be paid by all for the expenses of the league into the treasury established on the sacred island of Delos, but Athens had full control from the beginning, as the collectors were all Athenian officers. The virtues of this unification were great for the tributary states but greater for Athens, which effectively had under its control a vast fleet for use in war. In 454 the mask of equality was dropped when the treasury was moved to Athens and the members became virtually subject-states. Thus was born the Athenian empire.

Originally the right of secession was enjoyed by all members, as the notion of empire was contrary to the essential of Greek political thought, namely that each state was an independent unit. This defiance of Greek political morality rankled in the breasts of freedom-loving men and, when the Thirty Years' Peace between Athens and Sparta was broken at its mid-point, the rest of Greece took sides. From that moment, the Athenian empire was doomed.

The opening chapters of the history contain the remarks of Thucydides on the legendary beginnings of Greek history. The whole of "The Archaeology" makes three points, only the first of which is suggested for discussion in this "Great Book."

1. Settled life and material progress become possible only through political unification and forcible control by some central authority. Thus the nomadic life of the early Hellenes was not conducive to the formation of stable cities; and it was only when Athens, having poor soil and hence being undesirable and uninvaded, grew in population and prestige that progress and power could be achieved. This is Thucydides' first principle: the significance of power in the history of civilization.

2. The significance of naval power in the history of Greece: the state with the most powerful navy would inevitably rule Greece and, since large navies demanded large crews, there is a connection between naval supremacy and democracy; in fact, Themistocles and Pericles, both navy-minded, were leaders of the Popular Party.

3. The importance of stable government: Sparta was strong because of the rigid framework of her institutions, while Athens

was weakened by the looser democratic structure of the state. Nevertheless, as a land-power, Sparta was outmoded, and the logic of Greek history demanded that the vigor and self-confidence of Athenian freedom should have made her the mistress of the Greek world. Athens failed to hold the mastery because Athenian politicians were false to the principles of Pericles.

The immediate spark that started the conflagration was a minor dispute between Plataea and Thebes. Theban prisoners, taken after a "sneak attack" on Plataea, were summarily murdered in spite of, according to Thebes, the Plataean oath that they would be returned unharmed. Athens came to the aid of its ally Plataea, which denied there had ever been any oath. Greece reached a fever-pitch of excitement at the prospect of a death struggle between its two most powerful cities; contradictory oracles were received from the gods and an earthquake at Delos was taken to be vastly significant. The general opinion of Hellas was favorable to Sparta, which appeared as the champion of liberty against the tyrannical domination of Athens. The war continued for nine years, with Athens scoring victories in which its fleet could give it dominance, and Sparta hacking away at the land side of the Athenian allies. The second year of the war had seen the disastrous plague in which thousands died in an over-crowded Athens.

At this time the success of the enterprising Brasidas, the most un-Spartan of Spartan generals, had the Athenians in a state of utter discouragement; and they were all too eager to listen to the pleadings of the Peace Party of Nicias, although Athens was in no position to sue for favorable terms. At Sparta, too, weariness of war and a feeling that their successes would win them advantageous concessions from Athens caused the government to move in the same direction. Besides, Pleistoanax, the king who had been lately restored from exile, was worried by persistent rumors that his recall had been managed by bribing the priestess of the Oracle at Delphi, and he believed he could quash such charges forever if he negotiated a successful peace.

A truce of a year was arranged and was kept, except in Thrace; at Amphipolis was fought a battle which resulted in victory for Sparta but in the death of Brasidas, and of Cleon, the strongest opponent of peace in the Athenian Assembly. Sparta had no one who could carry on the gains of Brasidas, and Nicias was prepared to sacrifice the empire of Athens for the sake of peace. The temper of the people demanded an end to war and, since Athens fought with a completely citizen army, democratic opinion was triumphant.

The peace was not accepted by some of the most potent allies of Sparta, and a subsequent change in the political leadership in both states boded ill for its duration. Hardly a year passed before Athens joined Argos in an expedition against Epidaurus; Sparta hastened to the aid of its ally, and Athens declared that Sparta had broken the peace. The most powerful advocate of war at Athens was Alcibiades, a young man of brilliant intellect (he had been an associate of Socrates), noble birth and not a shred of morality. He was loved and followed, or feared and courted, by the varying factions in Athens; as a relative of Pericles he had been trained for statecraft, but the defects of his unstable character produced merely an unscrupulous politician; he was a man involved in democratic processes without the slightest respect for democracy, and he became the evil genius which was to destroy Athens.

Alcibiades was the main influence in the decision of Athens to send an expedition to Syracuse, and his speech to that end is the fourth of the sections of this "Great Book." Nicias had spoken against any overseas expansion at a time when things at home were in none too safe a state. As a moderate, he was promptly labeled "reactionary" by the young and impetuous radicals, led by Alcibiades. His call to caution served only to inflame the enthusiasm of the imperialists and, when he tried to frighten them with an analysis of the magnitude of the men and supplies needed, they gladly voted an even larger subsidy.

Moderation was defeated the moment Alcibiades rose to address the Assembly. His speech is a marvel of sophistry in which he plays, with half-truths, on the vanity and complacency of the Athenians. Sicily, he assured them, would be an easy prey to Athenian might and, as Athens owed all her greatness to a policy of expansion, she must now continue or forever be false to her destiny, and the slaves of some other conqueror. It was a case of a dominant personality against a hesitant weakling, and democracy always loves an adventurous gambler. And, as if Athens were proving the saying "Whom the gods would destroy, they first make mad," the control of the expedition was entrusted to Alcibiades, who soon went over to Sparta and to Nicias, who believed the whole idea to be utter folly.

Never before had so magnificent or so costly an armament been sent out by any Hellenic power and never was there to be so complete a disaster. Treachery, military and naval ineptitude, carelessness and extremely bad luck—all contributed to the catastrophe that spelled the end of Athenian power. Pericles had died in the third year of the war but, before his death, he had warned the Athenians that if they were patient and never sought to enlarge their dominion while war was going on, they would be victorious. Nothing could have been so thoroughly contrary to Periclean policy as the mad dream of empire beyond the seas that was the Sicilian Expedition. The war dragged on for another ten years, but Athens was never again the mighty power she had been. If this was not perceived at home, the truth was seen by the leaders of some of the Ionian allies of Athens and it is with this, the beginning of the revolt of the members of the collapsing Confederacy of Delos, that the last selection deals. At the urging of Tissaphernes, the Persian satrap of Sardis, the revolt began at Chios and was soon followed by other island and coastal states. Sparta made a treaty with Persia, handing over to it the Greek states of the Ionian coast, and Persia was to support the Spartan navy for the duration of the war. It was an end and a beginning: from now on, the Persian king was to be the arbiter of the affairs of Greece.

If we take our cue from Thucydides, who believed that history would repeat itself in future ages, profitable discussion of the Peloponnesian War must naturally focus on the following ideas:

1. Political power as an impetus to progress and material progress as the matrix of power.

2. The influence of personal feuds and party differences on the determination of democratic decisions.

3. National pride and complacency.

4. The danger of deterioration of voluntary union into involuntary servitude.

5. The precarious stability of an empire based on force.

EDWIN A. QUAIN

SELECTED BIBLIOGRAPHY

FINLEY, John H., *Thucydides*. Harvard University Press.
BURNET, John, *A History of Greece*. Modern Library.
JOWETT, Benjamin, trans., *The Peloponnesian War*. Oxford.
THUCYDIDES, *History of the Peloponnesian War*. Random (Modern Library).

Aristophanes: Lysistrata, Birds, Clouds

WHEN THE throngs from all Attica gathered in Athens in ancient times for the annual festival in honor of the god Dionysus, the groundlings doubtless endured the heavy and lyrical tragedies with a hope of amusement in the comedies that traditionally followed. Each was presented in a series of competing dramas, and prizes were awarded for the plays that, in the popular estimation, were the best. Among the greatest of the Comic Poets was Aristophanes whose *The Clouds, The Birds* and *Lysistrata* form the contents of a "Great Book" for modern reading and discussion. Whereas tragedy took the ancient myths for its subject and reveled in the glamorous past of Greece, comedy was intensely modern and topical and enjoyed the utmost freedom of abuse and caricature of the follies and evils of the times. When we recall that Athens of the fifth century was by any standards a small town, the effectiveness of a medium that held up to ridicule all levels of the Athenian citizenry can readily be visualized.

The humor of Aristophanes is occasionally that of situation, but generally he stresses caricature of well-known persons and, at every turn, local allusion, frequently sharpened by incongruity. He had an unerring eye for the precise weakness that would present his victim in the least impressive light, and his general purpose, apart from sheer amusement, might be said to be an attempt to curb the abnormal tendencies of his times in education, politics and private life. His career extended all through the Peloponnesian War and for some sixteen years after it and a large share of the barbs of his wit is aimed at the fumbling and bickering of politicians trying to pose as statesmen.

It would seem almost inevitable that the satirical turn of mind is an exclusive quality of conservatives. Rarely, if ever, do we find an effective satirist as an apostle of new ideas; generally, they look back on the hardy old days and the primitive virtues and bemoan their absence in the lesser men of their own times. It is a question that might well be discussed whether comedy was and is the creator of public opinion or merely reflects its prevalence and vigor at any given time. It would seem most likely that Aristophanes, despite his undoubted political prejudices, was merely a more acute observer of the contemporary scene with the energy to put his ideas before the public.

Athenian comedy as a whole did not have any noble ideal to preach and it never formulates a plan of action, which should not be too surprising since we must recall that every citizen of Athens was a potential Senator. As an ordinary citizen of Athens, Aristophanes aimed to please his own class; nothing gives greater pleasure to a democratic crowd than a telling hit at one of the great men of the moment, particularly if he has made his mistakes. The Comic Muse has ever looked on men and movements with a slight squint, and the mirror held up to nature always carries some distortion. For all the vigor of his attack on the follies of his times, Aristophanes was proud of his city and of her achievements; in the prime of his life, Athens, with all its defects, was the greatest state of the ancient world.

Since the days of the Homeric heroes the Greeks admired the art of persuasive speech and, with the rise of democracy, the ability to express oneself on political and ethical questions was of paramount importance. Normally, any lawsuit (and the Athenians appear to have been the most litigious people ever to have lived) had to be argued in person by the plaintiff and defendant. Hence the importance of the techniques which the "Sophists" claimed to teach. These men were the most striking manifestation of the speculative and slightly skeptical attitude of the times, and they played their part in the vigorous intellectual ferment of Periclean Athens. History, however, has been largely unkind to them in stressing their excesses; for this Plato and Aristophanes are much to blame.

When scarcely out of his teens, Aristophanes wrote *The Clouds*, a brilliant satire on the Sophists and the New Education. While ideas are traditionally hard to ridicule, the caricature of a well-known person is easy, especially when even the kindest interpretation of a character would label a man as eccentric. The most prominent of the Sophists were all foreigners, and their wildest pretensions, the fallacious tricks of the art of rhetoric and Ionian investigations into the secrets of nature, all lent themselves admirably to the humor of the comic poet. For his target, Aristophanes chose Socrates, a man known to every Athenian.

What mattered it if Socrates was comparatively mild in his strictures on the traditional theology? Or if he condemned at every turn the shallowness and chicanery of the more extreme practitioners of rhetoric? For the ordinary man, Socrates was a troublesome character who refused to be silenced by men who mouthed the traditional lore without either understanding or believing it; and his persistent questionings and peculiar mode of life among a people who worshipped success in wealth, politics and war, made him the ideal butt for comedy. All the defects of the Sophists were rolled into one man and presented for the amusement of Athens.

The harried father of a horse-playing son is at his wits' end to pay his debts until he learns that the Sophists can teach a man how to talk his way out of any predicament, and he hies him off to the "Thinking Factory" of Socrates. There the Master is found swinging above the ground in a basket, the better to investigate the secrets of the heavens untrammeled by the distractions of earth. His disciples in various undignified postures are delving into the mysteries below the earth and among the stars. The old man, Strepsiades, enrolls and is taken under the tutelage of Socrates, who finds him unspeakably dull and incapable of learning even the ridiculous nonsense that is apparently the basic course of the school. He is taught to deny all the gods, reserving that title for the Clouds (who form the Chorus) from whom all blessings come. In desperation, the Chorus suggests that he bring his wayward son Pheidippides to school; perhaps *he* may be able to learn.

For the instruction of the younger man, Right Logic and Wrong Logic are introduced and debate with each other. Right Logic stands up for all the traditional virtues and morality and pleads for the allegiance of the boy. Wrong Logic in turn tells its tale and advocates every brand of vicious immorality. All too well does Pheidippides learn his lesson; after the creditors have been dispersed, he turns his ready wit and facile arguments on his father and proves (by word and deed) that it is his right to beat his parents. In complete disillusionment, Strepsiades reverts to his former views and burns down the "Thinking Factory."

At the appearance of *The Birds,* some nine years later, Aristophanes found Athens in the full glow of enthusiasm at the launching of the Sicilian Expedition. His purpose in this play is far from clear, and the most that can be said is that he is reflecting the mood of the Athenian people with a rather mild (for him) satire on political and theological questions. Perhaps, however, he was hinting at the folly of an elaborate course of imperialism at a time when the home-fires definitely needed tending.

In any case, he portrayed two old Athenians, whom he calls Plausible and Hopeful, departing in disgust from Athens under the guidance of a Jay and a Raven, two potent birds in soothsaying. They are led to the lair of the Hoopoe, formerly the Athenian named Tereus, but now a bird. With him they discuss the founding of a City of the Birds. He calls a conference of all the birds, who are at first hostile, but, soon calmed, agree to the founding of Cloudcuckooland, midway between earth and heaven, where birds will be kings and gods, and the former gods, deprived (by the intervening city) of their incense and the odor of sacrificial meats, will die of starvation. The two men are transformed into birds, and the commonwealth is under way.

The various tasks are assigned to the birds and, with marvelous rapidity, the walls of the city begin to rise in the thin air. This is, of course, facilitated by the presence of storks and crows who can, hod on shoulder, fly to the top of the walls and lay their stones. The news of the new foundation spreads and a poet, a soothsayer, a geometrician and a lawmaker apply for admission, only to be summarily kicked out by Plausible who wants none of the plagues of Athens in his city. The gods begin to notice the coolness of men and send ambassadors to sue for peace, but not before Prometheus—an atheist from the beginning—apprises Plausible of the pitiful state of the gods and advises him not to give in to their demands; rather he must demand the restoration of the Birds to their rightful state and, for himself, the maiden Sovereignty as his bride.

The embassy arrives while Plausible is giving orders for the cooking of a dish of wild fowl (Birds who have been executed for high misdemeanors); and Hercules, who on the way had been all for violent attack on the usurpers, succumbs to the aroma of the savory mess. Complete capitulation to the demands of Cloudcuckooland follows and Hercules stays to see that the food is not spoiled. Meanwhile all Athens has become bird-conscious, and applications for citizenship are pouring in. The play closes with the arrival of Plausible in a splendid car, with his bride at his side, and carrying the thunderbolts of the great Jove in his hands.

The disastrous failure of the Sicilian Expedition on which Athenians had based their hope of an overseas empire left them in a state of despair and in a mood of war-weariness which clamored for an end to hostilities. It was at this point that Aristophanes brought out his comedy, *Lysistrata*. Since the men of Athens had done such a poor job of settling their differences with Sparta, Lysistrata calls a parley of the women of Greece to end the war. The plan is that the women will leave their husbands, neglecting their families and homes till peace is made. As a first step, the women seize the Acropolis and the Treasury of Athens, since obviously without silver no war can be waged, just as there would have been no war at all, were it not for the insatiable desire for that metal. The men attempt to storm the citadel and set fire to its walls, but both the fire and the men are vanquished by the sturdy ladies of Greece. Some faint-heartedness among her cohorts is rudely repressed by Lysistrata and finally, just when the ties of domesticity are asserting their claim, word comes that Sparta is in an equally bad state and envoys arrive from both warring cities. When hostile recrimination begins to control the negotiations, Lysistrata, with Reconciliation at her side, composes all differences in compromise. A feast is held for all; husbands and wives are reunited and the play ends with a dance and songs from all.

This mere skeleton of the comedy can convey no idea of the gross obscenity of its contents; the play is singularly lacking in restraint either in situation, dialog or stage directions. Fortunately, translations have concealed most of the double meanings but, entirely expurgated, the play would have little point. Even the current bowdlerized versions are far from fit reading for most minds. Great Books readers therefore will be afforded ample material for discussion of the rights of realism in literature and its relation to morality. One is inevitably reminded that, although the roots of Western culture lie in the literature, art and philosophy of ancient Greece and Rome, there are some elements that stem exclusively from Christianity.

Enthusiasm for the great ancients should not, therefore, becloud one's vision of the staggering gulf that lies between pagan amorality and the Christian ideal of purity and holiness. Socrates could plead with apostolic zeal for the pursuit of justice, but it was an ideal that left much to be desired.

One might suspect that Aristophanes was chosen for a place in the series of Great Books by way of comic relief. However, profitable discussion might well center on his significance in crystallizing public opinion in a democratic state, with modern parallels, his value as an exponent of free speech, as a critic of political chicanery, and as a source for the history of ancient times.

EDWIN A. QUAIN

SELECTED BIBLIOGRAPHY

BURY, J. B., *A History of Greece*. Modern Library.
MURRAY, Gilbert, *A Study of Aristophanes*. Oxford.
ARISTOPHANES, *Birds, Clouds*. Dutton (Everyman's Library).

Aristotle: Ethics, *Book I*

IN reading Aristotle's *Nicomachean Ethics,* one must realize how great an effort is needed, in a period of philosophical decay such as ours, to free oneself from the prejudices, intellectual fashions and distorted concepts which, unconsciously absorbed like disease germs, bar us from real understanding of a classic philosophical work.

Only if we succeed in escaping the present unfortunate climate of subjectivism, relativism, positivism and all the other modern "isms," in elevating ourselves to the level of the problems at stake and in obtaining a direct contact with the realm of being which is discussed here, shall we really profit from the study of this work.

In reading such a great classical philosophical book, our approach should, moreover, unite a respectful willingness to reach an authentic understanding of the author's thought with a deep and sincere thirst for truth. This thirst for truth is an indispensable prerequisite for any real understanding of Aristotle. Only if interest in truth has priority over a quasi-esthetic enjoyment of the "greatness" of the work, only if we contemplate it under the aspect of objective truth and not merely of its immanent intellectual power, only then can we do justice to a great philosophical work and appreciate the author's real contribution.

The first thing which strikes us while reading the *Ethics* of Aristotle is that it embodies the genuine philosophical approach: 1) in it we find the always fresh effort to maintain immediate contact with reality, the capacity to listen to being, which enabled Aristotle to develop an incredible variety of problems; 2) we are struck by the caution with which he proceeds, the awareness that this is but a first contact, the fear of premature standardization of his theories; 3) Aristotle unites a deep respect for former great philosophies with an implacable thirst for truth and the courage to correct a traditional view, if truth compels him to do so. This attitude finds expression in his criticism of Plato.

But what is even more admirable, Aristotle does not let himself be imprisoned in his own theses; he prefers to violate consistency rather than close his eyes to reality in order to save the integrity of his system.

We should not, therefore, exclusively consider the main theses of the ethical inquiry of Aristotle and judge his works according to them. We must equally take into account the many deep insights which at times flare up "by the way"—insights which often shatter the frame of the main thesis and surpass it in depth of vision and conformity with reality.

Finally, we should realize that the value of a philosophical work is determined not only by the true answers it may present to a problem, but also by the character of the problem posed.

Aristotle begins his *Nicomachean Ethics* by inquiring whether there exists a chief good, and what the nature of this chief good is: a classical problem, into which every true system of ethics must inquire—what is objectively the most important, most precious, most noble thing, that which embodies the highest value and which we should prefer to everything else? Whether Aristotle is right or not in introducing finality as the way to discover this chief good can certainly be discussed. Whether the criterion of the chief good really consists in the fact that every object of our will and desire must be intended as a means for it, may be doubted. The hierarchy of values and goods must certainly be distinguished from the relation of means and ends.

According to Aristotle, happiness is the chief good, because it is in view of happiness that everything else is sought. Obviously this statement remains vague so long as the nature of true happiness is not defined. After refuting several previous definitions, Aristotle arrives at a concept of happiness which culminates in the words: ". . . for we have practically defined happiness as a sort of good life and good action." We must concede that Aristotle here surpasses any merely subjectively oriented concept of happiness, in that he finds the determining mark of true happiness in the goodness and nobility of an activity—that is to say, in its objective value.

But, more than merely basing happiness on the good, Aristotle admits here that the *value* of what is morally good does not derive from its function as a means to happiness—a typical case of his philosophical independence of his own abstract theses. In a detailed analysis, his immediate contact with being takes precedence over the immanent logic of his previous theories.

We find another such flash of deep insight surpassing the level of the rest of his analysis in the words: "The man who does not rejoice in noble actions is not even good." Aristotle here grasps the fact that the moral ideal does not demand only conformity of our *will* with objective values, but of our *heart* as well. The antithesis to Kant's exclusive alternative of duty and inclination is obvious, for to love that which is good implies a higher degree of morality than to conform to it with our will alone.

The question then arises: "Does a virtuous life in itself suffice to guarantee happiness?" In contradistinction to the Stoic's pride, Aristotle's answer breathes sober thought and a deeply human spirit: "Happiness implies also the absence of great sufferings, and the possession of goods in addition to the virtuous activity of the soul."

A further flash of deep insight is expressed in the sentence: "Yet even in these [sufferings] nobility shines through, when a man bears with resignation many great misfortunes, not through *insensibility* to pain, but through nobility and greatness of the soul." Stoic *apathia* is not the mark of the noble man, but rather the enduring with resignation those pains which are deeply experienced.

Any discussion of the first book of Aristotle's *Ethics* should certainly stress his powerful concentration on the classical problem of the chief good, the concept of *eudaimonia* which implies and presupposes the idea of objective value and which is opposed not only to hedonism but also to the different modern eudaimonisms with their exclusively subjective standards.

Aristotle's insight into the legitimate role of happiness in the ideal of a perfect human existence may best be appreciated by comparing it with Stoic pride and Kant's exclusive alternative between duty and inclination. But, above all, we should stress the difference between Aristotle's *Ethics* and the Christian concept of the aim of life. The authentic link between happiness and morality can never be found in a mere world-immanent concept.

The cornerstone of Christian morality as expressed in the words of Our Lord, "He who loses his soul will gain it," is the *love of God for His own sake,* and the partaking of God's love for our neighbor.

DIETRICH VON HILDEBRAND

Aristotle: Politics, *Book I*

THE WORK of Aristotle which has come down to posterity under the title of "Politics," and which proved to be so tremendously influential in shaping Western political philosophy, was not written at one time and probably not even in the order of the books that now stands, though this order apparently was established by Aristotle himself. From the penetrating study by Werner Jaeger (*Aristotle; Fundamentals of the History of His Development.* Oxford, 1934) it seems definitely clear that when Aristotle began to write on matters political he first followed the tradition handed down by Plato and wrote a description of the ideal state or a "Utopia," although his ideal was quite different from Plato's. That idea is contained in Books VII and VIII. To this he wrote as an introduction what are now Books II and III—a critical survey of existing political theories, containing sharp attacks against Plato's views (II) and a discussion of what is to be regarded, according to Aristotle, as a presupposition for the constitution of states—the city and the citizen (III).

Later, with his interest growing in the historically given types of states, Aristotle discussed also actual political life too and not only the ideal state. He had at that time the great collection of constitutions made by the Academy at his disposal. Using this empirical material he gave his famous division of constitutions according to the participation of the citizens in the rule. Books IV-VI deal with these topics.

Finally, to this body of writing Aristotle prefixed Book I in which he discusses what he considers the elementary sociological and economic components of political life: the family-household and the village. Actually this introduction deals chiefly with two topics: the natural character of the state (chaps. 1, 2) and slavery (chaps. 3-13).

Basic in the first two chapters are the famous thesis that "man is a political animal" and the doctrine that the state aims at the highest good. Both belong intrinsically together. Man is a living being ordered towards a life in society. He is fully himself only when a member of society. His highest good, the good life, cannot be obtained where chaos prevails and where men act towards each other with brutal injustice. In all this Aristotle really touches upon the foundations of human existence.

By saying that the state aims at the highest good, Aristotle expresses the evident and important truth that order in the mutual relations of men is presupposed for human happiness. But beyond this he even points towards the truth that the highest good cannot be such as to be obtained by men living in isolation. But what is this highest good? It transcends earthly life, and that Aristotle did not see. If there is a "highest good," there must necessarily be a society directed towards it, but this the state never can be. Such a society can only be what Saint Augustine 700 years later called "The City of God." Through divine revelation we know that the perfect society directed towards the highest good is the Church, for the highest good is eternal beatitude. We also can grasp the fact that such a society and such a good alone fully correspond to the nature of man, and that man would be a tragic failure in his innermost aspirations if the state were the highest society and earthly happiness the highest good. Aristotle's greatness here lies in the fact that he points in a direction where truth greater than he can grasp is mysteriously hidden.

Aristotle stresses the organic growth of the state out of human nature and natural human situations. The profound point, however, is that he distinguishes his "political animal" most clearly from the gregarious brute. Men can spiritually communicate by speech, and this is a unique human feature; man "alone has any sense of good and evil, of the just and the unjust," of moral values. "But only the association of living beings who have this sense makes a family and a state."

These statements contain implicitly a vigorous refutation of the totalitarian concept of the state with its oppression of a free communication of thought among the citizens and the disregard of the "sense of good and evil," innate in human nature. It is indeed the decisive question whether citizens are treated by the rulers as gregarious animals or as persons, i.e., spiritual beings who respond to and are responsible for values. In the passage that follows there is another deep insight. Man is the only living being that can fail, while the other living beings do nothing but realize their own natures. "Man when perfected is the best of animals, but when separated from law and justice, he is the worst of all; since armed injustice is the more dangerous." This anticipates the famous Augustinian saying: "If justice is removed, what are kingdoms but big gangs of robbers" (*De Civitate Dei* IV, 3).

So the true state, in a way, liberates man to himself by ordering human social relations in justice. "Justice is the bond of men in states: for it is the administration of justice, i.e., the determination of what is (*in concreto*) just, which is the principle of order in political society." This positive concept of the state as of an institution destined to help man to his well-being by helping him to live in justice was most influential up to the time of the Renaissance, when the concept of the state began to be treated negatively in the writings of Machiavelli, Hobbes and Luther. It was then that the science of politics was no longer regarded as a branch of morals.

The extended discussion of slavery which follows and takes up the rest of Book I must deeply disappoint everyone who would expect at least the great philosophers to take exception to the common acceptance of slavery in antiquity and to its justification as a social and economic necessity.

Aristotle's thesis "that some men are by nature free, and others slaves and that for these slavery is both expedient and right" is therefore by no means something original. But his arguments for the support of it are interesting, for Aristotle subjected the legitimacy of the means of getting slaves (war and piracy) to some sharp criticism by pointing out that victory is not always with the greater virtues; yet he gives a rational justification to the institution as such.

What prevented him from breaking through to the discovery of the "self-evident truth" (not always followed even by those who hold it to be such) "that all men are created equal," was on the one hand the ancient concept of manual labor as being unworthy of a free man and, on the other hand, the experience of factual inequality, too easily interpreted as making people fall readily into clear groups of inferior and superior beings. The deeply rooted prejudices of society, the pride of the cultured Greek freeman looking down on the barbarian, were liable to render the apparent distinction still sharper and more definite.

Here is the important point: the equality of man in his basic rights and his basic dignity, although it is in itself a natural truth, was in fact only dimly recognized by the Stoics. It was only fully discovered after men were seen in the light of revelation as being equal before God, because created in the image of God, sharing with their fellowmen in the same misery of sin, redeemed in the blood of the God-Man, called to mutual love in Christ and expecting the same eternal beatitude. Only in this light does the natural dignity of man become, so to speak, "co-visible."

One of the more immediate effects of the Christian doctrine and practice was that manual labor no longer was considered a disgrace. But not only that: the nobility of service as such was discovered. Aristotle is right with his argument: there must be service. This in fact belongs to the human situation. But this is an argument for slavery if one is bound to the ancient approach to manual labor as Aristotle was. So he could conceive of service only as of something to be enforced and could, therefore, not escape the conclusion that slavery must be. The slave was for him a means and had to be treated as a means. By accepting this consequence, Aristotle became blinded to the dignity of man as it is rooted in his very nature, for wherever man is treated as a mere means, his dignity is most deeply violated.

The question of service is in fact as important for a full understanding of the problem of slavery as is the equality of men. But how could Aristotle have seen what was still to come as a *real* experience: the nobility of the service of those who enjoy "the freedom of the children of God," even if their social status be the most humble. How could he have seen that such service and the humility it presupposes, are not only compatible with the dignity of the human person, but even one of its deepest sources, paradoxical though it may seem. The revelation of Christ, who said of Himself that He came "not to be served, but to serve," was necessary to enable man to discover this truth.

Thus the first book of Aristotle's Politics is one great demonstration that man needs revelation in order to come to an understanding of himself, even of what he is by nature; and it is also a demonstration of the truth that true humanism needs to see man in the light of what transcends man.

BALDUIN V. SCHWARZ

SELECTED BIBLIOGRAPHY

NEWMAN, W. L., *The Politics of Aristotle*, with an introduction, prefatory essays and notes, two volumes. Oxford.

JOWETT, Benjamin, *Aristotle's Politics Translated*. Modern Library.

BARKER, Ernest, *The Politics of Aristotle*. Oxford.

JAEGER, Werner, *Aristotle; Fundamentals of the History of His Thought*. Oxford.

COPLESTON, Frederick, S. J., *A History of Philosophy*. Volume I: Greece and Rome. Newman Bookshop, Westminster, Maryland.

BARKER, Ernest, *The Political Thought of Plato and Aristotle*. London.

ARISTOTLE, *Ethics*. Random (Modern Library).

Plutarch: Lycurgus, Numa and Comparison; Alexander and Caesar

WE KNOW very little in detail of the life of Plutarch save that he lived in the first century of our era, being born at Chaeronea in Greece and educated in Athens; that he traveled throughout the ancient world, lived for a time in Rome and ended his days in literary leisure at the shrine of Apollo at Delphi. The man who wrote the lives of so many prominent figures of Greece and Rome found no one who undertook to write an account of his own career. This is probably "poetic justice," since Plutarch himself apparently did not consider mere literary figures worthy of immortalization in his works, restricting himself to those who had distinguished themselves in public life.

A born hero-worshipper, Plutarch applied his undoubted literary gifts to the portrayal of the rulers, leaders, soldiers and statesmen of the Mediterranean world. In his day, Greece had long been a vassal state of the mighty empire of Rome and, with the undying patriotism of a Greek steeped in all the heroic lore of ancient Hellas, he did not wish the world to lose sight of her former glory. For Greece in her hour of submission was forgetting her great men of action, harking back to her men of thought, while both were in danger of being overshadowed by the mighty exploits of the city on the Tiber whose empire then surrounded every shore of the Mediterranean (*mare nostrum*) and extended as far into the interior as stubborn nature and barbarous tribes would permit the progress of her legions. To right this balance, Plutarch strove to tell the story of the giants of *action* of his native land.

Fifty lives in all have come down to us from the pen of Plutarch, generally arranged in contrasting or similar pairs; for most of these, he himself has supplied us with a "Comparison" in which, as a matter of fact, he outlined for us the similarities that existed between the characters of the heroes of Greece and Rome.

This spectator of the life of Man chose to write biography and not history. We shall look in vain for an exhaustive account of the career of his hero; Plutarch has chosen those exploits which make his characters live. To this end, he will digress from the progress of his story to embroider a glamorous tale that will illustrate the glory of his subject. An incurable romancer, Plutarch preferred the picturesque detail, the mysterious or miraculous incident, the fabulous story of primitive grandeur, to the more prosaic drabness of a workaday world. Dramatic incident and intriguing anecdote make each figure shine forth clearly from his pages and if the resulting picture belies the findings of more sober historians, the cause is to be found in his lack of true historical insight and understanding of the political background in which his heroes moved and had their fabulous being.

For this "Great Book," four figures have been chosen: two mythical lawgivers and two outstanding commanders. The names and persons of Lycurgus and Numa are so heavily enshrouded in the mists of antiquity that, were it not for Plutarch, we should hardly know more than their names. The exploits of Alexander the Great and Caesar have been immortalized in history, but their individual personalities are living and vibrant only in Plutarch's romantic account of their foragings over half the earth. With unbounded capacity for searching out details, he has gathered together all the stories that surrounded these famous names; many a reader will be surprised to find that old Plutarch is the source of the tales we learned as children.

While Bury, in his *History of Greece*, may hazard a guess that Lycurgus never existed, for Plutarch he has the actuality of a contemporary. Carefully his ancestry is outlined, and the most intimate thoughts which guided him in molding the Spartan temperament and constitution are clear as crystal. Finding Sparta a loose and frivolous state, he determined to apply to it his experience of other polities, and deliberately set about its reform. To achieve a process of equilibrium, he inserted the Council of the Elders as a "control" on the "feverish kings" and as a balance between the two catastrophes of tyranny and unbridled democracy. To this end, he redistributed all property, making each share equal to eliminate an aristocracy of wealth and substitute that of "virtue."

To restrain the acquisitive desires of human nature, he banished all "liberal" arts, retaining only such as contributed to the military nature of his state. Further, he banned all silver and gold, made money of iron, so heavy in weight and so trifling in value that deflationary stability was the perennial objective of Spartan economy. The common mess hall provided for all, and vigorous athletics were obligatory for boys and girls alike. Rigid regimentation of family and social life effectively smothered all personal affection or ambition, and the Spartan citizen lived only for the state while the state existed only for military efficiency.

To maintain the purity of this Spartan ideology he forbade foreign travel, lest acquaintance with other decadent states corrupt his people's assurance of the perfection of the Spartan way of life. Partly for the same reason, foreign artisans and traders were barred, since Sparta had nothing to sell and wanted no frivolous luxuries from outside. Helots performed all menial and merely useful tasks, and the citizen had extensive leisure to devote himself to training for war.

So rigidly restricted were all activities that the citizen of Sparta was no less a slave to the demands of the state than the despised and defeated helot. The greatness of Sparta is attributed by both Lycurgus and Plutarch to its adherence to this, "the best of all constitutions," according to the official pronouncement of the oracle.

In the shadowy figure of Pompilius Numa, Plutarch crystallizes the opposite process by which a vigorous and war-like people, the Romans, were gentled and weaned to the uses of peace and tranquillity. Accepting the kingship with reluctance, Numa, with the aid of a probably fictitious goddess, organized the life of Rome along religious, economic, political and social lines. No less than his Spartan analog, Numa regulated all details of life in Rome by persuading his subjects that divine guidance dictated every change in their hitherto lawless existence.

Numa is considered to have had the harder task—that of taming the vigorous spirit—while Lycurgus was constrained to spur a people dedicated to luxury. In both states simplicity and frugality of life were assured by legislation, and all luxuries and extravagances were banned. Personal initiative and individual desire were apparently subjugated with ease; while Sparta adhered to the laws of Lycurgus, she remained great according to Plutarch's standards and, curiously, the grandeur of Rome arose when she deserted the peaceful admonitions of Numa. Righteousness as defined by law was the creed of democratic Rome, and the same official justice was the law of aristocratic Sparta.

The uncritical objectivity of Plutarch is manifest on every page of these biographies. He was clearly enamored of genius that achieved success, and he never adverts to the fact that the methods and objectives of his heroes were in complete disregard of the autonomy of the individual. Since true freedom is based on the principle of personal worth and an individual immortal destiny, of which the pagan world was largely ignorant, the dominance of the omnipotent state could not but be assumed as valid.

Even clearer still is this attitude in the parallel lives of Alexander and Caesar. With his wonted enthusiasm for the marvelous, Plutarch strongly hints that the birth of Alexander was in some way miraculous. The frugality and self-control (in some lines) of the youthful Macedonian prince win his admiration, and he is happy to recount his association with Aristotle. The poems of Homer were kept under his pillow at night, and he was devoted to his horse, Bucephalus. Alternate kindliness and savage brutality mark his military career, in which he subjugated Asia from Greece to the Ganges. His superhuman courage and endurance won for him the fanatical devotion of his soldiers; the key to Alexander's character is found in his craving for glory, since "he loved his reputation more than his life or his kingdom."

Since Alexander and his father, Philip of Macedon, were considered by Greeks to have been barbarian despoilers of Hellenic liberty, it is striking to find Alexander almost begging for the admiration of the Athenians, to whom he wrote: "Can you possibly believe the perils I am undergoing to win glory in your eyes?" Plutarch's portrait of Alexander shows a gradual deterioration of character by which he falls from the pinnacle of the "Philosopher King" and demands the fawning adulation he had observed at the courts of oriental monarchs.

In the figure of Caesar, Plutarch finds a counterpart of Alexander. Tracing his career from his crucifixion of his former pirate captors as a youth, to his death at the feet of Pompey's statue, he outlines a character of inflexible ambition, utter unscrupulosity for the attainment of predetermined ends, uncanny political insight and the persevering diligence that made him the head of a powerful faction in Rome.

Many anecdotes are adduced to illustrate Caesar's courage, his generosity even to his enemies, at times his bloodthirsty cruelty, his tactical and strategic genius and his love for the dramatic gesture. In the pages of Plutarch we are witnesses to the fateful day when Caesar, pausing in thought by the river's bank, at last spurred his horse and crossed the Rubicon. The last days of his life were ready-made in dramatic form for Shakespeare, who turned to Plutarch for the story of his *Julius Caesar*.

Since the choice of these four biographies as a "Great Book" was obviously made with an eye to modern parallels, the field for discussion is provided with abundant material. The attempted extermination of whole peoples by both ancient and modern tyrannies will naturally lead to questioning in the matter of progress. In the course of centuries, mankind has learned a great deal as to the control of inanimate nature, but apparently very little in the way of curbing the selfishly immoral tendencies of human nature. When divine grace, freely given but of necessity to be freely accepted, is refused, modern man is no farther from the beast than his most primitive, unregenerate forebears.

In these lives, plentiful details are provided for the discussion of the theory and practice of the totalitarian state; the development of the lust for power and domination; the possibility of human happiness under a government that demands every loyalty to the destruction of freedom; cruelty and slaughter in ancient and modern times.

Much could also be said of the character of Plutarch himself as manifested in his writings. The gaps in his structure of morality are fearsome indeed. While his admiration for clemency and generosity is very great, he has no words of condemnation for unlimited slaughter, marital infidelity, perjury, suicide or drunkenness. In general, his attitude toward objective moral standards is fairly impartial; whatever his hero chose to do, for whatever reason, is for him right and just and, consequently, admirable. His worship of success quite effectively biinded him to the lack of moral stature in his heroes.

EDWIN A. QUAIN

SELECTED BIBLIOGRAPHY

BURY, J. B., *A History of Greece.* Modern Library.
TORN, W. W., *Helenistic Civilization.* Arnold, London.
TYRRELL, R. Y., *Essays on Greek Literature.* Macmillan.
PLUTARCH, *Lives, the Dryden Translation.* Random (Modern Library).

7

St. Augustine: Confessions, *Books I-VIII*

You CANNOT get the best out of the *Confessions* if you know nothing of Augustine save what he tells you there. Indeed, you would not even learn his name, for it is not mentioned anywhere in the book. But that is a trifle. What matters is that he has no conception of his own greatness or of his towering importance in the history of mankind. So that one might read it simply as the spiritual story of an able, pious man—it hardly matters who— living at some time in the past—it hardly matters when.

Reading it thus, one would miss too much of the significance. For the man who is here baring his mind and his soul to God and to us is one of the key figures of all history. "He was," says the Catholic historian Christopher Dawson, "to a far greater degree than any emperor or barbarian war lord, a maker of history and a builder of the bridge which was to lead from the old world to the new." The great liberal Protestant scholar Harnack writes as forcibly: "It would seem that the miserable existence of the Roman Empire in the West was prolonged until then, only to permit Augustine's influence to be exercised on universal history." In reading the *Confessions,* you are not reading the diary of a nobody. Every man living in the Western world would be a different man if Augustine had not been, or had been different. Naturally Augustine did not know this, but it is a pity if we do not.

Observe the moment. He was born in Africa, one of the mightiest provinces of the Church, in 354—forty years after Constantine had the dream or vision which swung the Roman Empire to Christianity. He died in 430, with the Vandals, who had wrested Africa from the Roman Empire, hammering at the gates of his episcopal city. It was the age of the dying of the Empire in the West and the passing of power to the Barbarians. The Empire had long been administered in two parts, with an

Emperor in the East and an Emperor in the West: in 392 (the year after Augustine became a priest) Theodosius, the Eastern Emperor, became Emperor of the West as well. He died in 395, the last man to rule the whole Roman world. With his sons, the division was restored. The Eastern Empire, based upon Constantinople, was to last for another thousand years. The Western Empire fell to the Barbarians in a lifetime.

For Western civilization (which ultimately means ourselves among others!) the break was immense. It meant two things. In the secular order, the new rulers were men to whom the ancient classical tradition meant nothing. In the ecclesiastical order, the new situation meant the severance of the West from the East— the hierarchical unity lasted some centuries longer, but the old closeness was gone: and it was in the East that practically all the great theological thinking had been done. The Western world started on its new career under the double threat that civilization would be cut off from the Classics, that the Church would be cut off from its intellectual sources.

It did not happen so. It was Augustine who made the difference. "Single handed, he shifted the center of gravity," says Father Martindale. In himself he summed up and by his prestige gave to the new Europe all that was richest in the Classics: for the educators of the new Europe were to be the monks: and the monks took their curriculum from Augustine's treatise *De Doctrina Christiana* (not from the *Confessions,* where he dismisses the Classics pretty cavalierly). What he did for theology was even more remarkable. For in him—just at the moment of its most urgent need—the Western Church produced its first enormous intellect. Firmly, profoundly, *in Latin,* he stated all the great Christian truths: above all the doctrine of the Trinity, the supreme truth about God, and the doctrine of grace, the supreme truth about man's way to God. With the social order crashing about his ears, he went to the fundamentals of soul and society. His reaction to the sack of Rome by Alaric in 410 was to write *The City of God:*

Two loves had built two cities—love of self to the despising of God had built the earthly city; love of God to the despising of self, the heavenly city.

Or as he says in his Commentary on Psalm 64:

Two loves make up these two cities: love of God makes Jerusalem, love of the world makes Babylon. Let each question himself as to what he loves, and he shall find of which he is a citizen.

To write a book seemed a pitiful way to meet a catastrophe so vast, but the book laid the foundations of a Christian sociology; for Charlemagne, four hundred years later, it was a kind of Bible; more than any other single influence it shaped the Middle Ages. And just as Charlemagne was taught by *The City of God,* so two hundred years before him Gregory the Great in his mighty reform of the Church was nourished by the *Confessions.* By the twelfth century, first-rate thinkers were once more in action in the Church. But for the seven centuries between, the one light that shone steadily was Augustine's.

If you would know why this one man could throw his influence so far across the centuries, the *Confessions* will tell you. He was a genius, of course, and genius carries. But we can get closer to his secret.

To begin with, there is his personality. Reading the *Confessions,* you realize that you have never met a man even faintly like him. He joins the Church at the age of 33: twelve years later he writes the *Confessions.* By now he is a bishop, and he writes of himself with an unaffected candor that would be startling in a bartender.

Nor is he writing only of past sins, now happily conquered: it is a great pity that students should stop at Book VIII and not get the marvelous analysis of his present spiritual state in Book X —no one could read that section and not feel that Augustine is unique among the great. And uniqueness carries.

Then there is his power with words. You will meet with examples on every page of the *Confessions*; and remember that you are reading only what a wretched translator could make of them in English: the Latin is immeasurably more striking. No philosopher ever made such phrases, and great words carry.

For a third thing, there is his psychological insight, into himself and others. We could not have arrived at his psychological findings, but once he utters them we can check them from experience: they are dead right, and rightness carries.

But the heart of his secret is that his philosophy comes at us winged with passion: he was a passionate man, and the passion poured into his teaching not to muddy or confuse it but to give it impetus. He gives us his teaching and he gives us himself with it. In the experiences of life he learned certain truths: he does not skim the truth off the experience and give us that; he gives us the truth in the concrete experience in which he learned it. He gives us not the result only but the process. The problems he states are real problems, they have given him years of anguish. The solutions then had to be real solutions. Colored water will cure an imaginary illness, but genuine disease needs a genuine remedy. When he tells you how he came to dominate (not eliminate, you notice, only dominate) sexual temptation, you know that he had really been tortured by it. And all men of turbulent passions recognize him for a brother.

What gives the *Confessions* their special quality is that Augustine was a passionate man with two passions not often found at such intensity in the one man: there was his bodily passion for women, which came to him with adolescence, and his intellectual passion for truth, which seems to have come a few years later with the reading of Cicero's *Hortensius.* A clamorous body and a clamorous mind both demanded satisfaction, and he could not silence either for the other. What the body wanted was simple enough. What the mind wanted was truth about God (especially how could He be everywhere unless He Himself had spatial dimensions); and it wanted the truth about God both because it was the primary truth and it was the condition of having any other truth at all.

And, as a problem that took in both the others, he saw that he must consider the origin of evil. He had come to know the sexual tyranny as evil: could God be the creator of evil? And if so, must He not be evil Himself? The Manichaeans and their heresy held him for nine years: it should have soothed the conflict in him, for it taught that evil had a separate creator over against God; and that the evil in himself was another will distinct from his own, and implying no guilt in him. But his intellect was not satisfied; he was totally incapable of the faintest intellectual dishonesty; he could not shirk a problem. Convenient for his own special case as their teachings were, he came to know them for false.

The book will tell you what he did about his three problems. He came to see that evil was not being but non-being, not something but the absence of something that should have been there:

and as such it could not have a creator. Painfully he came to the truth about God: that He is pure spirit with no material element, and that He is in all things not by similarity of dimensions but by superiority of power. But with this came a new problem: how could God have become man, which meant uniting matter to Himself—for matter was surely a principle of degradation? And at last he knew the truth, that spirit has the primacy of matter, but that matter has its own sort of sacredness, too.

Don't dream that all this is an academic problem, suited to a fourth-century professor, but for us only a historical curiosity. It is the literal truth that this twin doctrine of matter's sacredness but spirit's primacy brought the Dark Ages through into the order of the great Middle Ages. It is the doctrine that our own age needs most urgently. It brought that world out of chaos and could bring our world out of chaos, too. Nothing else can. Further, it gave Augustine the mental framework within which he could see the truth about sexual appetite and, by God's grace, bring it under control. And in the matter of sex, our own age is as deadly sick as ever Augustine was.

FRANK SHEED

SELECTED BIBLIOGRAPHY

D'ARCY, M. C., S. J., and others, *A Monument to St. Augustine*. Sheed and Ward.
PRZYWARA, Erich, S. J., *An Augustine Synthesis*. Sheed and Ward.
DAWSON, Christopher, *The Making of Europe*. Sheed and Ward.
HUGHES, Philip, *A History of the Church*. Volume II. Sheed and Ward.
ST. AUGUSTINE, *Confessions*. Dutton (Everyman's Library).

8

St. Thomas: Treatise on Law

IN THE very early days of radio the old crystal sets made it exasperatingly possible, within a few moments, to hear a few bars of music, a few sentences of an oration and a few blows of a prizefight. Of course, no one argued that it was possible, under these circumstances, to appreciate the music, to follow the argument or to predict the outcome of the fight. This, however, is precisely the mistake made by the student who reads the tract on law by St. Thomas as a Great Book. It is not a Great Book; it is a fragment smack out of the middle of a very great book.

This tract on law from the *Summa Theologica* must be seen as a fragment, read as a fragment, under pain of misunderstanding the tract itself. The book from which it is taken has for one of its outstanding characteristics a perfect ordering of its thought. What is to be found in the very middle of the book is there of set purpose; which is to say that it couldn't, in the profound opinion of the author, be put any place else, because all that has gone before is essential to the understanding of this particular tract. For this tract to make sense, then, the basic truths that precede it in the *Summa* must at least be seen as basic in the thought of St. Thomas.

The appearance of law on the stage at the end of the second volume of the *Summa* becomes intelligible only when we have seen, in the first volume, an infinitely perfect God creating a world of spiritual, material and human creatures, all moved to the divine ends of the world by a divine government respecting the created natures which it is moving to their goals. We will have focused on the human creatures and seen man as a composite of body and soul, endowed with intelligence and free will, to whom physical force is a violation of nature, and moral force alone the movement consonant with his nature. This human creature must be seen as lifted far above his natural powers

and natural goals by divine grace, and equipped for supernatural living on that supernatural plane; but fallen from it
through a mysterious perversity that still characterizes the world
of sin. In common with the pure spirits, this human creature is
capable of receiving direction and, in his turn, of giving it; for
he is in a true sense a participant of the providence and government of God, a creature made not so much to be moved as to be
ordered, and to command his own obedience.

The second volume establishes the fact of a goal commensurate
with the intelligence and free will of man; then accepts a supernatural goal more proper to God than to man. The instruments
by which man attains to this goal will be his own acts—acts
which have for their outstanding characteristic that of being controlled, directed, dominated by man himself. From this there
follow the solid notions of morality, of responsibility, of reward
and punishment; for all of these flow from the very nature of a
controlled action aimed at or away from a goal. In the natural
order that goal will be the reasonable good, the good that
responds to the rational nature of man; in the supernatural order,
where alone man's life is a success or a failure, that goal is no less
than the eternal vision of God.

After a thorough inspection of these controlled actions in
themselves and in their principles—man's passions and good and
bad habits—we are ready to look to law for guidance and to
grace for help.

There are several points in the tract on law in St. Thomas for
which the reader, approaching it for the first time, might well be
prepared. Among these may be mentioned: the deceptively compact definition of law; the analogous character of Eternal Law;
the double puzzle of Natural Law's obligation and nature; and
the field of positive law, both human and divine. A brief word
on each of these points will make up the rest of this article.

In defining law, it is to be understood that St. Thomas is
speaking of the law formally, i.e., as it exists in the mind of the
legislator. He is not immediately concerned with law as it exists
in codes of law or in the understanding of the subjects who must
obey that law. In this sense, Thomas reduces all law to an
authoritative, effective directive motion to a goal. His exact
words are: "Law is a dictate of reason for the common good promulgated by one who has care of the community." In other

words, Thomas has traced law to the common action of the controlling faculties of all human action, to intellect and will, thereby forever joining action and truth; whims, caprices, wilfulness are ruled out by truth, while sterile intellectual gymnastics are eliminated by action. The goal of good is the only excuse for the existence of law; and since a common good belongs to the community rather than to the individual, it is only the community, or its vice-regent, that can give authoritative direction. Promulgation, of course, is a necessary condition for observance of the law on the part of the subjects.

This definition follows from the very nature of man, who can be directed but must not be coerced. In all the physical universe, man is the only creature who can have law in this strict moral sense, because he alone has intelligence and free will; on the other hand, he is the only creature who needs law, because he is the only one who is not driven by necessity but who chooses his own path by actions which are under his control.

When we speak of law in God we are talking in terms of analogy; God is utterly simple, in Him all things are one. The distinctions we make, the terms we use, are after our own mode of knowledge; since our intellect is so very feeble we must break up the white light of divinity lest it blind us altogether. This being understood, it is clear that an infinitely wise Creator, ordering the world to His divine ends, is by that fact a legislator. We must, then, see in divinity a divine dictate of reason ordering all creatures to the common end of the world. Since everything in God is eternal, this dictate of reason, or law, is eternal, even though it could be promulgated to creatures only in time.

In the *Summa Contra Gentiles* (Book III, chaps. 80 and 97) St. Thomas pushes this inquiry to its uttermost depths: the Eternal Law is that dictate of divine reason which determines the essences or natures of things. From this determination, all the details of divine providence and the divine government follow as conclusions from a principle. The basis of all law, then, is the truth of things as they are; the moral order and the ontological order are inextricably intertwined. Morality is truth in action. Whatever the fluctuations, variety or progress of law, this unchanging basis of truth is the solid, permanent foundation on which the lives and societies of men can be built securely.

This Eternal Law is promulgated by the Natural Law, or the

participation of the Eternal Law in creatures, the law that is written by the finger of God in the very nature of things. Here, obviously, the discussion will be of law as it is in its subject rather than in the legislator; though, in the spiritual and the human world, there is a sense in which the creatures are themselves legislators, participating in the legislature privileges of God, with the result that the Natural Law in them lives up strictly to the generic definition of law. It must also be clear that a sharp distinction must be made between the Natural Law that guides inanimate and brute creation to their ends and the Natural Moral Law by which a man's conscience is bound, whatever the vagaries of his feet and hands. The Natural Law, in the sense of physical laws driving the elements, the plants, the animals and the physical side of man under the whip of necessity, cannot really be fitted into the definition of law properly so-called. This is not law, but it is so called in an improper, almost metaphorical sense. Law, strictly so called, is found in the natural order only in the world of spirits and of men; and there it is always a Natural *Moral* Law.

The first difficulty about this law in men arises from the fact that human nature is complete from the first instant of life, while a dictate of reason is possible only after some years. How can there be law, i.e., a dictate of reason, in man from nature from his first instant of life? How can a law be called natural that makes its appearance only after several years of life have passed? With an almost excessive brevity, St. Thomas meets the difficulty by distinguishing the three component parts of the Natural Moral Law in men: 1) the natural inclinations which are in man from the first instant of life—a kind of passive participation of the Eternal Law which he has in common with all the rest of creation; 2) the faculty of reason, by which truth can be recognized—a kind of passive participation of the Eternal Law which is proper to man himself; 3) from these two, when the age of reason is reached, there follows, *necessarily and immediately*, a dictate of reason— an active participation of the Eternal Law in man by which he participates in the government of his own life and the life of the world, providing for himself and others.

This dictate of reason is unintelligible as natural without the natural inclinations and the faculty of reason. These latter two are unintelligible as law, however natural they may be, without the dictate of reason. It is precisely in the dictate of reason that the Natural Moral Law is formally located. This dictate of reason can be variously phrased: "follow your inclinations," "act for your end," "do good, avoid evil." All of these say exactly the same thing. From this first and most universal principle there follow as immediate conclusions the secondary precepts of the Natural Moral Law, the precepts that correspond to the Ten Commandments—and more remotely, with much more chance of ignorance and error, the tertiary precepts of the Natural Moral Law will also follow as conclusions from a principle.

To this law a man is bound, and knows he is bound, whether or not he ever comes to a knowledge of the existence of God. The sanction of the law is the very essence of things, the very nature of man; the law in man is a cause, though a secondary cause, of the obligation which is the inevitable secondary effect of all law. It is not that a man obliges himself, but rather that the reason of man, echoing the order of divinity, cannot deny the good, however corruptly his will may reject it. In pursuing evil, he violates his human nature, turns aside from his human end; and knows that nature will exact its punishment.

Human positive law is a necessity because of the infinite details of human life and the very general character of Natural Moral Law. Not that this positive law adds to the Natural Law, or increases the weight of its sanctions; rather it further *determines* the universal precepts of the law from which it takes its rise. A positive law, for example, forbidding murder is really not a positive law but an authoritative repetition of a command of the Natural Law; on the other hand, the determination of specific titles to ownership is strictly positive law. Positive law, in other words, does not create obligations where none existed before, but from a variety of means by which an existent obligation can be fulfilled, it chooses, or determines which one, in fact, must be used. Positive law presupposes good and evil, i.e., the necessary relationship of this act to this end—it does not establish these things.

Over and above this essential limitation of positive law to the *determination* of the Natural Law, there is a further and no less obvious limitation of positive law to the external acts of man; a limitation that does not hold for the Natural Moral Law or for the divine Positive Law, precisely because both are divine and the heart of man is the proper territory of God. Where all citizens are vicious, it is simply impossible to expect results from human positive law; it is absurd to expect sanctity as a fruit of human positive law when it can do no more than regulate the external actions by which men come into contact with one another. Its field is to keep the peace and further the common good of the community; its order is temporal, external, for political ends.

Ordinarily we think of divine Positive Law in terms of the Ten Commandments. In that sense, the divine Positive Law is an explicit restatement of the secondary precepts of the Natural Law, made necessary by the feebleness of intellect and weakness of will on the part of men. Actually, the divine Positive Law goes far beyond this, embracing the supernatural precepts of Christ and reaching to the supernatural goals of man, which belong properly to God. Sharing something of these divine prerogatives is the ecclesiastical Positive Law, at least in the supernatural and eternal character of its goals, and its jurisdiction over the thoughts and desires of the hearts of men.

Whatever their particular character, all laws must find common ground in their ultimately divine origins, and in their beneficent design of guiding man to the end where alone he can fulfill his nature and the supernature which is his gift from God.

WALTER FARRELL

SELECTED BIBLIOGRAPHY

The *Summa Theologica* of St. Thomas Aquinas: Ia 2ae Par., Qq. 90-108. Benziger.

FARRELL, W., *The Companion to the Summa.* Vol. II, pp. 365-414. Sheed and Ward.

FARRELL, W., *The National Moral Law according to St. Thomas and Suarez.* B. Humphries.

ROMMEN, H. A., *The Natural Law.* Herder.

LEIBELL, J. F., *Readings in Ethics.* Loyola University Press.

KREILKAMP, K., *The Metaphysical Foundations of Thomistic Jurisprudence.* Catholic University Press.

CHROUST, A. H., Collins, F. A., "Basic Ideas in the Philosophy of Law of St. Thomas Aquinas as found in the Summa Theologica." 26 Marquette Law Review 11-29, Dec. 1941.

DE WULF, M., *History of Medieval Philosophy.* Longmans Green. Vol. II: *Philosophy of St. Thomas.*

SERTILLANGES, A., *Philosophie des Lois.*

ST. THOMAS AQUINAS, *Selected Writings.* Dutton (Everyman's Library).

Niccolò Machiavelli: The Prince

MACHIAVELLI'S MOST famous work is a great book, and like most
—or should we say all?—great books, it comes from a great
tradition. It is a strikingly original book, but it is not a mere
novelty or a literary and philosophical *creatio ex nihilo*. It would
not have been written unless many men before Machiavelli had
written on the state and statecraft and on the ideal commonwealth and the ideal ruler. If Plato had not written *The Republic, The Laws,* and *The Statesman;* if St. Thomas Aquinas
had not written *De Rege et Regno;* if the whole literature of "the
mirror for princes" had not gone before him, Machiavelli could
not have written *The Prince.* He belongs to the tradition, not because he continues it, but in the sense that he breaks with it and
does his part to frustrate it.

As with every work of art, it is important in the case of *The
Prince* to know something, or better, to know as much as possible, about its efficient cause. Niccolò Machiavelli was born at
Florence in 1469.[1] The career in public life that he chose for
himself had periods of prosperity and of misfortune. He made his
way to office and responsibility during the turbulent years at the
end of the century when Savonarola rose to power and fell from
it. He was a successful administrator and a skillful diplomat, but
like so many others in public life, Machiavelli's tenure of office
was insecure. He had to contend with both malice domestic and
foreign levies. Thus the defeat of Florence at the hands of Pope
Julius II in 1512 resulted in Machiavelli's loss of position and
afterwards in his imprisonment for suspected complicity in a
plot against the Medici. The remaining years of his life were
spent in disfavor and retirement, but they were the years in which
he did the work upon which his fame rests. Before his death in

---

[1] For the life of Machiavelli see Pasquale Villari, *La Storia di Niccolò Machiavelli
e de' Suoi Tempi.* Florence, 1877-82; English translation by Linda Villari, London,
Unwin, 1892; also the article by Umberto Benigni in the *Catholic Encyclopedia.*

1527 he had written his *Discourses on the First Ten Books of Titus Livius, The Art of War, The History of Florence,* some biographical studies, various literary works, including three comedies, the most famous of which is the brilliant *La Mandragola,* poems, and stories, some familiar letters, and *The Prince.*[2]

During these years of exile from the courts of princes, Machiavelli did not despair of returning to favor and office. Nor did he disdain to plead his cause and otherwise strive to regain the notice of the great. *The Prince* itself is an instance of this, as is revealed in its dedication to Lorenzo the Magnificent, son of Piero de' Medici. Machiavelli offers to him not "horses, arms, cloth of gold, gems, and such-like ornaments,"[3] things that other suitors for favor hold dear or that they think will delight a prince. Machiavelli offers what he himself holds dearest and esteems most highly. This is his "knowledge of the deeds of great men," which he has acquired through long experience of contemporary events and constant study of past history. It is no mean gift, for it will enable Lorenzo the Magnificent to learn in a short time what the author learned only "at the cost of privation and danger in the course of many years." To follow its injunctions, Machiavelli adroitly implies, will raise Lorenzo to that grandeur which fortune and his own merits presage for him. In reward it is asked only that Lorenzo gaze down from his lofty height and recognize "the great and unmerited sufferings" inflicted on the author by a cruel fate.

Written at the time of the high renaissance, *The Prince* is one of the books that have helped to form the modern mind and to shape the course of modern history. Because it is such a book, it is not strange that it can be described in terms that are operative words in our society: it is realistic and it is practical. Its author has been a man of affairs, and he is always the shrewd observer and the candid commentator. In the modern manner, he is interested in facts rather than in principles, although from his facts he will draw conclusions that in their turn will become principles. He is fully aware of "the novelty and gravity" of his

[2] Guido Mazzoni and Mario Casella, editors, *Tutte le Opere Storiche e Letterarie di Niccolò Machiavelli.* Firenze, G. Barbèra, 1929.

[3] All quotations from *The Prince* are from the translation by Luigi Ricci, revised by E. R. P. Vincent, Oxford, Humphrey Milford, 1935, and New York, The Modern Library. *The Prince* is not now listed in the Church's *Index Librorum Prohibitorum,* as is sometimes thought, although it was condemned by Pope Paul IV in 1557.

subject. He writes of "the states and dominions that hold sway over mankind." His book is about the men who hold sway over the states and dominions and it is for them.

Since it is Machiavelli's intention "to write something of use to those who understand," he thinks that it is "more proper to go to the real truth of the matter than to its imagination." He does not use or know the terms, but he repudiates both utopias and eutopias. It is true, he says, that others "have imagined republics and principalities which have never been seen or known to exist in reality." His own concern is not with such figments of the fancy. He is concerned not so much with how the ideal prince ought to act as with how real princes do in fact act in this real world. There is, he holds, so great a distance between principle and fact that the man "who abandons what is done for what ought to be done, will rather learn to bring about his own ruin than his preservation." Hence Machiavelli concludes that if a prince wants to maintain himself in power he must "learn how not to be good, and to use this knowledge and not use it, according to the necessity of the case."

In popular opinion, princes are praised for having certain qualities and blamed for having others. One ruler is lauded for being generous; another is condemned for being miserly. So also is the contrast made between the merciful and the cruel, the trustworthy and the faithless, the chaste and the lustful, the serious and the frivolous, the religious and the unbelieving, the courteous and the haughty, the craven and the brave. The common opinion is that it would be a good thing for a prince to have all those qualities which are considered good. Machiavelli does not agree. It is impossible for a ruler to have all these virtues, and the reason given is that human conditions do not permit it. It suffices that a prince should avoid those scandalous vices which would cost him his throne and to guard against those lesser vices which do not actually endanger his position.

Machiavelli distinguishes between certain real and certain apparent virtues and between the corresponding vices. For instance, every prince must desire to be considered merciful and not cruel. Yet there are times when a seeming mercy may cause great suffering; so also there are times when an apparent harshness can result in real good. Cesare Borgia had a reputation for cruelty, but it was a cruelty that restored peace and order to the Romagna. A right consideration of his conduct will reveal that he was in fact much more merciful than were the Florentines upon a certain occasion. In order to avoid reproach of cruelty, they allowed Pistoia to be destroyed. Similarly, a prince's generosity may exhaust a kingdom, whereas his thrift may make it strong.

A new prince, a man who is building up his realm by force and cunning, must be cautious in his plans and deeds, and yet at the same time he must be daring. Will it be better for him to be loved or feared? Machiavelli's answer is revealing: "One ought to be both feared and loved, but as it is difficult for the two to go together, it is much safer to be feared than loved, if one of the two has to be wanting." The reason is clear to one who has no illusions concerning the weakness and wickedness of human nature. In general, men are ungrateful, deceitful, cowardly, and covetous. They will promise anything—treasure, children, and life itself—but at the first chance they will revolt. Men have little scruple in offending a ruler who seeks their love, "for love is held by a chain of obligation which, men being selfish, is broken whenever it serves their purpose; but fear is maintained by a dread of punishment, which never fails." Even so, a prince should try to avoid hatred when he cannot gain his subjects' love, "for fear and the absence of hatred may well go together."

It is evident that Machiavelli is at times justified in making his realistic and practical distinctions between virtues and vices that are truly such and those that are merely apparent. Such distinctions are the commonplaces of moral theory and are required for the successful conduct of life. Machiavelli, however, goes beyond these legitimate and necessary contrasts and advances a doctrine that is a radical departure from the teaching of the traditional moralists. His eighteenth chapter is entitled "In What Way Princes Must Keep Faith" and in it he gives his essential thought its most explicit statement. It is this chapter more than any other that has lent to the adjective Machiavellian its familiar meaning.

For Machiavelli man is something more than the rational animal of the accepted definition. He indicates that there are in him two natures, that of man and that of the beast. Hence in war, the great art and science that must be the constant study of princes, there are two ways of fighting, "the one by law, the other by force: the first method is that of men, the second of beasts." In anticipation of von Clausewitz's maxim that war is only the continuation of national policy, Machiavelli holds that fighting "by law" is often insufficient and recourse must be made to force. Hence "the prince must know how to use both natures, and that the one without the other is not durable." A new metaphor is introduced. The prudent and successful ruler must be both the lion and the fox—the fox to recognize traps, the lion to frighten wolves. Rulers who think only of being lions do not understand this, and Machiavelli insists that the prudent ruler must also be the fox. Moreover, to be the fox, he must not keep faith when it is against his interest and when new conditions replace those under which he gave his word. "If men were all good, this precept would not be a good one; but as they are bad, and would not observe their faith with you, so you are not bound to keep faith with them."

Abundant instances could be provided to support this advice. There is "an infinite number of modern examples" that will show how often peace has been broken and promises made worthless by the deceit of princes. The fox has succeeded best, and he has succeeded best because he has been able to disguise his character as a fox. Not only are men bad, as Machiavelli has already indicated, but he indicates that they are fools as well: "one who deceives will always find those who allow themselves to be deceived." Hence the foxes have seen with Machiavelli that it is impossible and even dangerous to possess all the virtues. They have held that they should "seem to be all mercy, faith, integrity, humanity, and religion," but they have also held that they are "often obliged, in order to maintain the state, to act against faith, against charity, against humanity, and against religion." The successful prince will be ready to adapt himself "according to the wind, and as the variations of fortune dictate, and . . . not deviate from what is good, if possible, but be able to do evil if constrained."

The prince must have war as his constant study because the art of war is the only art that is necessary for him, whether in his rise to power or in maintaining his position. Since a neglect of this art is the greatest cause of loss of power, the wise prince will devote all his energies during peaceful times to preparing for conflict. Hence Machiavelli gives a part of his book to a consideration of military affairs. Among other things, he points out the dangers that follow from the use of mercenaries and foreign troops and contrasts with them the advantages that come from a native militia. In these chapters upon war and soldiering Machiavelli again shows himself to be a pioneer with regard to future developments in political theory and practice. He anticipates in his thought the organization of modern nations as war societies. His insistence that the prince's primary concern is with inevitable war and his concept of the secular ruler, exempt from the restrictions of religion and morality, are forerunners of ideas and facts that have become dominant in our own time. Nineteenth-century ideals of the nation in arms and twentieth-century realities, such as total war and the consolidation of military and political power in the hands of a single leader, would not have too strange an aspect to Machiavelli returned to earth.

If an abstractly ideal ruler is not presented in *The Prince,* there is in it one whom Machiavelli can "hold up as an example to be imitated by all who by fortune and with the arms of others have risen to power." It is the Duke Valentine, better known as Cesare Borgia, the son of Pope Alexander VI. He was a prince who did everything that a prudent and capable man could do in order to establish himself firmly in power. He fomented disorders in neighboring states; he weakened his rivals by bribing their adherents; he divided and conquered; he waged aggressive wars; he set a ruthless minister over conquered territory; he then slew the minister in order to ingratiate himself with the people. He took thought of the future "by destroying all the blood of those ruling families he had despoiled," as well as by other foresighted plans. Only one thing Cesare Borgia did not foresee, that at the greatest crisis in his career he himself would lie dying. Machiavelli does not moralize over this error, nor does he recall the words once addressed to a certain rich man: "Thou fool, this night do they demand thy soul of thee; and the things that thou hast provided, whose will they be?"

Consideration of Cesare Borgia's character and career leads Machiavelli to his conclusions of admiration and praise: "For with his great courage and high ambition he could not have acted otherwise, and his designs were only frustrated by the short life of Alexander and his own illness." As with individual princes, so with nations: success and failure are the only true

tests and standards of political conduct. If one state has the
power and the opportunity to overrun another, then that is
what it ought to do. It is to be condemned only for attempting
what it cannot carry through to a successful issue, or for receiving
benefits not justified by its own strength. "If France with her
own forces could have taken Naples, she ought to have done
so; if she could not, she ought not to have shared it." It is might
that makes right. More than that, for Machiavelli it is might
that makes duty. Here is a curious inversion of the Greek maxim,
that "Can dwells ever nigh to Must." Having denied that princes
can live completely good lives, the renaissance thinker asserts
that, if there is any question of morality in statecraft, it is the
exact reverse. For him, Must will dwell ever nigh to Can.

Machiavelli, therefore, has not been faithful to his original
purpose. He has not remained the impartial observer and the
unprejudiced reporter. In spite of himself, he becomes the moral
philosopher: he argues, this is what the prince ought to do. In
doing so, he illustrates anew how difficult it is for a man to be
a complete positivist. He shows how impossible it is to dispose
of all norms and principles, even if those that he at length accepts
are no better than superior force and deeper cunning. So also
his book illustrates anew how the philosopher of history cannot remain the mere realist. Almost as a matter of course, he
picks out his ideal prince and hero, and holds him up as an
example to be extolled and imitated.

Throughout the book there are many maxims touching upon
matters of statecraft that rulers of any period would do well to
ponder upon and observe. Thus in a situation fraught with
danger of war it is advised that a ruler should never allow a
disorder to take place in order to avoid war. If this is done "war
is not thereby avoided, but only deferred to your disadvantage."
For our own part, it is not difficult to offer modern instances that
will illustrate this wise saw. Machiavelli illustrates his point by
the political ineptitude of the French in yielding Naples to Spain
and the Romagna to Alexander VI, deeds, he claims, that resulted in France's ruin. He admires France because it is well
governed and possesses institutions that protect the liberty and
security of the king. Chief of these is its parliament, for it serves
the double purpose of checking "the ambition and insolence
of the great nobles" and of favoring and placating the masses of

the people. Machiavelli offers shrewd and acceptable advice on such subjects as the choice of secretaries, the advantages of a consistent and resolute policy, the necessity of rewarding merit, and the wisdom of encouraging commerce and agriculture. The prince will do well to perform some great work of internal administration and "in every action to obtain fame for being great and excellent." He will also do well to shun flatterers and those who offer advice without being asked, while always being ready to ask counsel from the wise and honest. In the end, however, it holds true that all wise counsels are "due to the prudence of the prince, and not the prudence of the prince to the good counsels received."

Machiavelli closes his book with a chapter that does not rightly belong with those that have gone before it. It is a plea for the unification and liberation of Italy that does credit both to his heart and to his head. It makes him a prophet of the *risorgimento* and gives him a place among the great names of Italian nationalism.[4] In this concluding chapter he rises to a far higher level of thought than in the rest of the book, and he speaks with a passion and eloquence that his earlier subjects could not arouse. Machiavelli pictures the condition of the Italian people as it was over four centuries ago. They are "more enslaved than the Hebrews, more oppressed than the Persians, and more scattered than the Athenians." His countrymen are "without a head, without order, beaten, despoiled, lacerated, and overrun." He does not again name his ideal prince, but he laments that "at the highest summit of his career he was thrown aside by fortune." Now Italy is ready "to follow any standard if only there be some one to raise it," and to "do honor to himself and good to the mass of the people." It is an opportunity that must not be let slip, so that "Italy may at length find her liberator" and the "fatherland be raised up."

It is evident that there is more than one difference between this impassioned plea and the principles and method used throughout the body of the book. Machiavelli has here ceased to be Machiavellian. He recognizes and describes evils that are great and numerous, and he wants them replaced by something

4 The inscription on Machiavelli's tomb, erected in 1787 in the church of Santa Croce in Florence, reads: *Tanto nomini nullum par elogium:* Of so great a name no epitaph is worthy.

good. He is no longer content with describing what princes do;
in the name of virtue he exhorts a prince and tells him what
he ought to do. He argues in behalf of spiritual and moral
realities: patriotism, honor, the exaltation of the fatherland, and
the common good. He invokes the name of God and of the
Church. He holds that a war waged for such a cause is just and
quotes the moral theology of the schoolmen: "Here is a just
cause; *iustum enim est bellum quibus necessarium, et pia arma
ubi nulla nisi in armis spes est.*" He calls not for mere power and
craft, but for peace and order and unity and freedom. When
Machiavelli does all this, does he reflect that much that he has
taught in his earlier chapters makes for division rather than
for unity, for slavery rather than for freedom, and for fear and
disorder rather than for that tranquillity of order which is peace?

There are various ways of looking at *The Prince* and they
may be reduced to three. A reader may be impressed by things
in the book that may be called accidental to it rather than by
what belongs to its essence. The fervent patriotism of the call
for a free and united Italy, the maxims of a prudent and successful statecraft, and the various valid judgments upon the deeds
and habits common to men can distract a reader from what
is of the essence of the book or lead him to discount the radical
character of Machiavelli's major proposals. In such a reading a
full appreciation of Machiavelli's basic theses is lacking. There
will be comparisons made between Machiavelli and certain later
thinkers and doers in the realm of *realpolitik,* and the conclusion
will be drawn that his opinions are mild and moderate and
liberal. This view may be termed a naive interpretation of *The
Prince.* It is at variance both with popular opinion, as expressed
from the time of its publication down to our own day, and with
the judgment of the closest students of the work.

A second view of *The Prince* is that of those men who share
the author's cynical judgment upon human nature. With his
eyes they look upon the vast throng of men not only as evildoers
but as fools as well. They hold that innocence and virtue are of
little worth and of no avail against the forces of evil, that evil
must needs be done, and that the end will justify whatever
means the lion and the fox may determine to use. This interpretation is that of certain powerful political theorists and men
of state who well understand Machiavelli's essential doctrine and

accept it for their own. There is a third view which is far
removed from that of those who make *The Prince* their vade-
mecum, although it too rests upon a correct reading of the book's
lessons. It is the judgment of those who have distinguished between substance and accidents in the work but reject its basic
and characteristic doctrines.

The Prince was written in 1513, when Machiavelli was forty-
four years old. He had the experiences of his own career, the
events of his era, the record of medieval and renaissance history,
and the writings of the ancients, especially those of Livy, to
draw upon for material for his reflections. Four centuries later
we are in a unique position to see the full import of his book
and the full effect of his doctrines when put into practice. For
modern history, and particularly the history of our own times,
has been one vast documentation of *The Prince*. The totalitarian
state, its embodiment in the dicators, the intensification of power
made possible by modern science and industry, the secular faith
in force alone, the banishment of religion from government, the
denial of natural rights and duties, the exaltation of the lie,
the extermination not merely of the blood of ruling families but
of whole races, classes, and groups that would provide rival
leadership—all these things and many others tell us that
Machiavelli was right to stress the distance between what men's
lives and deeds are and what they ought to be.

The modern situation tells us with equal force how false are
the conclusions that Machiavelli draws from this unhappy contrast between what men do and what they ought to do. We may
take his own pragmatic norm of success and failure. Our world
has been plunged into inconceivable disaster by new Machiavellis
and by new Caesars who have put the doctrines of *The Prince*
into practice. Is not this disaster the most vivid and irrefutable
commentary on the book? For if *The Prince* remains a great
book, it is not because of the depth and truth of its basic thought.
It is rather because of the greatness of its error and because of
the causal connection between its principles and the present
degradation of the human race.

JOHN K. RYAN

SELECTED BIBLIOGRAPHY

RICCI, Luigi, *The Works of Machiavelli,* translated and revised by E. R. P. Vincent. World Classics, Oxford.

LERNER, Max, ed., *The Prince and the Discourses.* Modern Library.

MUIR, D. Erskine, *Machiavelli and His Times.* Dutton.

GILBERT, Allan H., *Machiavelli's Prince and Its Forerunners.* Duke University Press, Durham, North Carolina.

PRAZ, Mario, *Machiavelli and the Elizabethans.* Humphrey Milford, London.

BUTTERFIELD, H., *The Statecraft of Machiavelli.* Bell and Sons, London.

BURNHAM, James, *The Machiavellians, Defenders of Freedom.* Day.

Montaigne: Selected Essays

MONTAIGNE IS an atheist; he is a deist, a Roman Catholic but not a Christian, a stalwart Catholic apologist, a rationalist, a thoroughgoing skeptic, a radical, an arch-conservative, a stoic, an epicurean, a great stylist, a negligent writer. All these opinions have been stoutly maintained by scholars and critics during the three and a half centuries that have elapsed since his death in 1592. The reason for this confusion lies, I think, in a fact that is almost always forgotten: that the *Essays of Montaigne* are essays.

Because of the great fame and favor Montaigne's essays obtained almost immediately, we have become so accustomed to the essay as a literary *genre* that we accept the word, as we do the terms "epic," "comedy" or "novel," without stopping to think what it means and how it came to be applied to the form we know. The *Concise Oxford Dictionary* tells us correctly enough that an essay is an "attempt (at)," but when the term is applied to the literary form, the dictionary virtually gives up and just says that it is "a literary composition (usu. prose and short) on any subject." Dr. Johnson comes closer to a real definition: "a loose sally of the mind."

Montaigne himself frequently puts us on guard against this limitation of his method. His book is

a record of diverse and changeable events, or undecided and, when occasion arises, contradictory ideas; whether it be that I am another self, or that I grasp a subject in different circumstances and see it from a different point of view. So it may be that I contradict myself. . . . If my mind could find a firm footing, I should not speak tentatively *(je ne m'essaierois pas)*, I should decide; it is always in a state of apprenticeship, and on trial *(en espreuve)* ["Of Repentance"].

These words, *essaierois, apprentissage, en espreuve,* should warn us sufficiently that their author is not to be pressed too hard, nor should his words always be driven to their ultimate, logical and sometimes absurd conclusion. This does not mean that he writes lightly on subjects to which he has not devoted serious attention. He is, on the contrary, a very thoughtful, well-educated, extremely intelligent man of extraordinary common sense, good practical judgment and excellent natural instincts, who imparts to us the fruits of his careful reflection.

Montaigne makes it clear in many explicit statements, however, that he has no intention whatsoever of telling his readers what to think or do: "Others form man; I describe him, and portray a particular, very ill-made one. . . ." ["Of Repentance"]. He does not believe in "lecturing . . . like a schoolmaster, which I cannot do (and I do not observe that those who can do so effect any real improvement. . . .)" ["Of Experience"].

He further elucidates his method in the same essay when he reminds us that

authors communicate themselves to the world by some special and extrinsic mark; I am the first to do so by my general being, as Michel de Montaigne, not as a grammarian or a poet or a lawyer. If the world finds fault with me for speaking too much of myself, I find fault with the world for not even thinking of itself.

This passage, among others, reveals the fundamentally serious purpose behind Montaigne's very complete self-analysis. He believes that each individual man contains within himself a résumé of the entire human condition, with all its possibilities of wisdom and folly, of virtue and vice. If, then, we examine any one man thoroughly in all his thoughts, emotions and actions, we shall learn a great deal about man in general, his nature and conduct, and be aided thereby in formulating conclusions to guide us in our own lives.

As Lincoln was to put it:

If we could first know where we are, and whither we are tending, we could better judge what to do, and how to do it. . . . (Address on June 16, 1858 to the Illinois Republican State Convention).

Montaigne was deeply and properly concerned with his examination of what we are and where we are, but only too little with "whither we are tending." Nor did he have the wisdom to remember, as did Lincoln further on in this same speech, that "A house divided against itself cannot stand."

For Montaigne is concerned exclusively with human wisdom, and examines our conduct in life, love and death without reference to any other light than that of our human reason and reflection. Sainte-Beuve would have it that he is "simply nature; civilized nature, but nature without grace." This is perhaps true of the book, but surely not of the man. Most scholars today are agreed that Montaigne was a sincerely believing and practising Catholic, but with the fatal qualification that, as Professor Zeitlin puts it in the introduction to his excellent translation of the *Essays* (Knopf, New York, 1934): "Religion as an inner light governing the relations of man with his Maker was outside the province of his interest" (p. ix).

Before we are tempted to cast the first stone at Montaigne for this, however, we might well ask ourselves whether he is in this respect so very different from the many of us who sincerely believe and practice, but resolutely keep God and religion in what we consider to be their place—in church of a Sunday morning, in a sickroom or on a battlefield, where need of Him is felt. Montaigne is not the only one who might well be somewhat embarrassed to recall St. Bernard's dictum that the true measure of loving God is to love God without measure. Unlike us, however, he did live in a world that had only recently left off being fervently and even mystically Christian. That this still living tradition, in combination with his assiduously regular religious practice (he was careful never to miss Mass, even when traveling, and often speaks of his prayers and confessions) and the lessons and prayers he heard in church, could not but influence the formation of his mind and conscience, even if only unconsciously.

That world of the Middle Ages, when the faith, however imperfectly observed, permeated all phases of human existence, drew to a close in a period of decadence, of terrible and widespread abuses and superstition, as well as of great holiness. Faith and reason, grace and nature were then closely intertwined, often to the great advantage of reason and nature, at the height of the Middle Ages, but too often also to their detriment or neglect, at the close. The explosion of the Renaissance, under the authority of the pagan classics, reasserted the claims of nature and reason, very frequently to excess and to the disparagement or neglect of grace and faith. An abuse of supernaturalism led almost inevitably to an equal or greater abuse of naturalism. Some

few great souls such as St. Thomas More or St. Francis de Sales
were able, with their immense gifts of grace and intellect, to
reëstablish a perfect equilibrium in their own lives and teaching,
but the damage had been done. Religion was felt to be hence-
forth apart from everyday life; God was put in His place. Let
Him not disturb us as we go about our worldly affairs during the
week.

Montaigne is a typical product of this mentality, which has
continued to set the tone of our civilization to this day. A man's
religion, we are told, is purely his private affair; it is no concern
of his fellow man what he believes, if he believes anything.
Montaigne tells us that

a wise man ought inwardly to withdraw his soul from the crowd and
preserve to it the liberty and power to judge of things freely, but
outwardly he should absolutely follow the accepted fashions and
forms. The public has nothing to do with our thoughts, but the rest
—our actions, our labors, our fortunes and our very lives—we must
lend and abandon to its service and to the prevailing view ["Of
Custom and that we should not Easily Change a Law Received"].

This passage and others like it have been interpreted as meaning
that Montaigne's public profession and practice of religion were
mere shams behind which he sought to shelter his audacious
attacks against that same religion. To maintain this view, one
must resemble the man Montaigne speaks of elsewhere, the man
who finds it impossible to believe that anyone can really think
differently from himself. The often-quoted passage above is
simply a hasty and injudicious expression of the two valid distinctions between the external and the internal forum, and between abstract truth and practical prudence.

We can, indeed, know a man only by what he shows of his
thoughts, his words and his actions; we cannot penetrate into
the intimate depths of his unrevealed mind. Likewise, it is
certain that we must deal with ourselves and with others as we
are, rather than as we think we ought to be. Montaigne himself
corrects this apparent assertion of the complete irresponsibility
of our private thinking in one of the numerous manuscript addi-
tions written in the margins of his copy of the *Essays* in the last
years of his life: "The true mirror of our doctrines is the conduct
of our lives" ("Of the Education of Children"). Our thoughts
and the teachings deriving from them are then very much a

matter of public concern, since they are the wellsprings of our conduct in life. Montaigne is extremely insistent throughout on the necessity of conforming our practice to our thinking and our principles, which thus become a matter of more than private concern.

In his extraordinarily keen and extensive examination of human nature and conduct in an infinite variety of situations and contingencies, Montaigne then proceeds in the light of human reason and judgment alone, without reference to revelation and faith. It is perhaps because of this that the *Essays* were placed on the *Index* in 1676. Since Rome does not explain its reasons in such cases, we can only surmise. It may be that the book was so condemned, not because of any error inherent in it, but because of its possible implications and the extreme errors into which it had led so many readers who conceived its author to be preaching irreligion. The historic use to which a book has actually been put is surely a legitimate consideration in estimating its influence.

It cannot be said, however, that Montaigne looked at nothing *sub specie aeternitatis;* he did, in fact, look at eternity itself under the aspect of eternity and he explicitly reserves an important place in his life for religion and its observances.

Our temporal life he considered only in itself and for itself. He similarly dissociated—and not merely distinguished between— reason and faith, giving to each authority in its own domain, but neglecting completely those processes of reason which may serve as preambles to faith. For, in all his use of reason and reflection on the problems of life, love and death, never once did he seriously address them to the fundamental problems of the existence of God, His veracity and the historical fact of a revelation, all of which are problems accessible to examination by human reason without the aid of faith. On the other hand, on the occasion of Montaigne's visit to Rome in 1580, his book was found in his baggage and was subjected to a most painstaking examination by the Roman Inquisition. The verdict was a general approval, although certain expressions were criticized as imprudent and unwary. Montaigne was thereafter well received and complimented by Pope Gregory XIII whose government subsequently conferred upon him the honorary title of Roman citizen. This papal honor awarded him after the examination of his book is evidence that during his lifetime it was found by competent Roman authority to be free from explicit error. Ninety-two years later, after the influence it exerted had been demonstrated, Rome decided that its reading could be harmful and it was accordingly placed on the list of forbidden books.

Montaigne was, on his own statement, a practising Catholic of scrupulous regularity who constantly reiterates his adhesion to the faith. There is no sound reason to doubt his word on this. Sainte-Beuve's picture of Montaigne as a sly sniper at religion, hiding behind a shelter of constant false professions, is completely out of character and contrary to Montaigne's fundamental hatred of sham, lying and every dishonorable action. This sentiment is so extreme and constant with him that Professor Zeitlin is led to attribute to him the opinion that "a man's honor and pledged word should be dearer to him than his own salvation or even than the salvation of his people" (p. xcii.). This is surely misleading if we are to understand by "salvation" man's eternal salvation. What is really meant is his temporal safety and welfare, and even here Montaigne expressly allows that a virtuous ruler may be regretfully obliged for reason of state (i.e., for the welfare of his people) to contravene his pledged word. And he even more strongly accords to moral principles precedence over the promise given:

In this case only does private interest justify us in failing to keep our promise: when we have promised a thing that is in itself wicked and iniquitous. For the right of virtue should prevail over the right of our obligation ["Of the Useful and the Honest"].

It is clear, then, that nothing contrary to our eternal salvation can possibly be binding on us, whatever promise we may have made.

In his consideration of the problems of everyday living in the light of natural reason alone, Montaigne proceeds from an early attitude of stoicism—which was more a literary pose than an intimate part of his character—to a moderate, but often apparently amoral sort of epicureanism in his later essays. He is, however, not to be taken too literally when he makes statements such as "I, who have no other aim but to live and be merry . . ." ("On some Lines of Vergil"), for that sort of "loose sally of the mind" is corrected by many other passages on the necessity of living according to one's conscience and honor, regardless of consequence or public opinion. Montaigne's conscience and honor were apparently not concerned with his enjoyment of the pleasures of life; these, it would seem, were controlled solely by his natural prudence and temperate inclinations. He is opposed to what he considered excessive or ascetic straining toward virtue:

> Virtue is natural and easy, it is beautiful, triumphant, loving, delightful and stout-hearted in equal measure, professed and irreconcilable enemy of bitterness, of unpleasantness, of fear and constraint, having for guide nature, for companions fortune and pleasure ["Of the Education of Children"].

Montaigne is then exclusively concerned with the natural viewpoint in his book, although he expressly reserves a place for the supernatural, in which domain he recognizes the authority of the Church without reservation. But once this territory has been conceded to religion, all the myriad circumstances of the conduct of human life, love, education and death are considered in the light of natural reason alone. Had he but followed the implications of his own insistence in his essay "Of the Education of Children" that

> It is not a mind, it is not a body that we are training; it is a man; and he ought not to be devided into two parts

to their logical conclusion that a man has only one mind and one life, not two, and that faith and religion can no more be dissociated from our daily life than the mind can from the body, he would have written a much wiser book.

It is true, of course, that an investigation of profound philosophical and social problems in the light of human reason alone is a perfectly legitimate undertaking. Boethius in his *Consolation of Philosophy* and St. Thomas More in his *Utopia* are examples of great Christians who have done so, but both of them in their other writings and their lives showed that their faith permeated their whole minds and was only dissociated from their natural reason for one specific enterprise. The case of Montaigne is quite different, since his book is the epitome of all his thinking.

He was, then, with this fundamental reservation, a wise man ("le sage, le trop sage Montaigne," Daniel Rops the contemporary French Catholic critic, calls him), one of good natural instincts and extraordinarily amiable character and mind which have endeared him and his book to endless thousands of readers since his day. His wide reading, keen insight into the human mind and his finely balanced judgments make his observations and comments delightful and instructive reading.

It is impossible to examine here the application of his two cardinal principles, "know thyself" and "follow nature," to the details of the conduct of life, but certain basic attitudes have, I hope, been established in the light of which Montaigne's *Essays* may be read with less danger of misunderstanding the final conclusions he would have us draw from them. For Montaigne is indeed one of the most dangerous authors in the history of literature when read out of context. There is no writer who lends himself less to being read in extracts; one essay, one passage, one thought must be corrected by another. They are, after all, just what he gave them out to be: trials, attempts, essays of his natural reason and judgment.

His lack of deep insight into spiritual things is a defect of his time and ours, but he lived, according to his lights, a good Christian, and he died an edifying death as he raised his eyes to the elevated Host at the Consecration during a Mass he had celebrated in his chamber in the presence of his family and neighbors in a last and solemn affirmation of his faith. The integrity of that faith is vouched for by his sharp observation:

> That which seems to me as much as anything to bring disorder into our consciences . . . is this partial yielding of their belief on the part of Catholics. . . . We should either wholly submit to the authority of our ecclesiastical government or altogether dispense with it. . . . Moreover, I can say this because I have made trial of it, having in former times used this freedom of private choice and election, treating as negligible certain points in the observance of our Church which had the appearance of being too unimportant or strange; coming to discuss them with learned men, I have found that these things have a very solid and massive foundation and that nothing but stupidity and ignorance makes us accept them with less reverence than the rest ["It is Folly to Measure Truth and Error by our own Capacity"].

Though he did not wish to be considered—and cannot be considered—a sure teacher of ultimate truth, there are still very many lessons of understanding, good sense, tolerance and kindness as well as high moral principles to be gathered in the pages of his book. Despite his easy-going manner and the endless digressions into which he is led by his never failing curiosity about the workings of the human mind and human customs, despite his numerous contradictions and easy tolerance of human foibles, his observations constantly lead him back to the lesson of reason and morality that

it is our duty to compose our character, not to compose books, and to win, not battles and provinces, but order and tranquillity for our conduct of life.

Our great and glorious masterpiece is to live to the purpose; all other things, ruling, laying up treasure, building, are at the most but appendicles and adminicles [the last of the *Essays*, "Of Experience"].

JEAN MISRAHI

SELECTED BIBLIOGRAPHY

ZEITLIN, Jacob, *The Essays of Montaigne.* (The introduction is of particular value.) Knopf.

BOASE, Alan M., *The Fortunes of Montaigne: A History of the Essays in France, 1580-1669.* Methuen.

FRAME, Donald M., *Montaigne in France, 1812-1852.* Columbia University.

MONTAIGNE, Michel, E. de, *Essays.* Dutton (Everyman's Library).

Shakespeare: Hamlet

IN APPROACHING a work of art in any field, one can obtain certain immediate and basic impressions, though, if the work of art is of a truly great order, these impressions will not be inclusive or subject to specific limitation. It is for this reason that a really great piece of literature is worth reading again and again, for one's changing experience and growth in life enable one to discover new insights and evaluations in it.

Such a work is *Hamlet* and, in approaching *Hamlet,* one is dealing with what is psychologically the subtlest work of a great genius, what J. Dover Wilson has called an "essay in mystery . . . so constructed that, the more it is examined, the more there is to discover." The most enigmatic piece of great literature in English is comparatively slow-moving (especially if insufficient emphasis is placed on the duel between Hamlet and the opposition led by Claudius), may even seem to drag in its latter part, and concludes in a litter of deaths and killings even more extravagant than those in *King Lear.*

But it is the intellectual dilemma of Hamlet's mind that gives the play its permanent excitement and more than compensates for any technical dramatic shortcomings, which raises the conflict above the melodrama that it superficially resembles. It is not the result of the surface stage action that is so important; rather it is the development of Hamlet's mind. As M. Roy Ridley states the matter: "What we want to know is not so much what Hamlet will *do* at the end of the play as what Hamlet will *be*. His actions matter in so far as they are an index of his state of mind."

Hamlet is a major work of art because of the depth and multiplicity of meaning contained in it. William Empson in his *Seven Types of Ambiguity* stressed the relevant point that great poetry assimilates many levels of meaning, that there is a relationship between the greatness of a work of art and the number of communicable, though not expressly stated, meanings it contains. In approaching *Hamlet,* especially, one should recognize the basic use that Shakespeare makes of ambiguity, both in the narrow sense of a specific dramatic method, and in the larger sense of an ambiguity whereby universal values are presented in a paradoxical way. It is more specifically evaluation rather than meaning that enters this larger sphere of ambiguity and, in this respect, I like to use the word, ambivalence.

By the deliberate use of ambiguity Shakespeare creates a specific kind of tension that has the validity of actual experience whereby we can foresee and foreshadow but cannot *foretell.* The ambiguity of many issues in this play (for example, the exact nature of the preternatural visitant, Hamlet's relations with Ophelia, the guilt or innocence of the Queen in regard to her husband's death) is a matter of concern to the characters themselves; it is the ambiguous issue that is part of the dramatic action, not its actual solution or condition.

This use of ambiguity, while outside and above Shakespeare's general procedure, is in harmony with it, for Shakespeare works in an impressionist manner, presenting characters fluidly in growth and movement, laying stress on contrast and irony. Such a procedure does not permit of the same surface perfection of form that a more static type of art might acquire. It is important to emphasize that Shakespeare works as a special kind of artist; he does not state a thesis; rather he makes a heightened imitation of life through specific techniques, of which the deliberate use of ambiguity is one of the most important to recognize.

The ambiguity and ambivalence of Shakespeare's method are partly explained by the historical circumstances of his theatre. Shakespeare was obliged to tell a surface story of conflict and climax that everyone could follow, whether he was an apprentice stealing away from his master's shop, or an erudite intellectual from an inn-of-court. It is clear from Shakespeare's own words in this very play that he placed primary value on the censure of the judicious and that he was aware of the problem familiar to the modern artist, that of presenting what is "caviar to the general." Shakespeare was fortunate in finding a working solution, that of keeping to the strong and simple outline of a story that was yet able to hold, within its sweep, complex and multi-dimensional meanings.

But the necessity of meeting and holding the attention of the "general" saved Shakespeare from that dangerous divorce (more particularly for the artist) wherein the intellectual subtlety of art is abstracted from a normal and popular means of communication and becomes a content and a form recognizable only by the privileged initiate and the coterie. Shakespeare's ability to combine both what is "general" with what is "caviar" makes his work more truly universal than, let us say, a coterie-sponsored book such as James Joyce's *Ulysses*.

Both *Hamlet* and *Ulysses* constitute psychological explorations; both have as an indirect objective the ascertaining of whether life has meaning; both penetrate the darker depths of the human mind. Both are ambiguous. But in Shakespeare the ambiguity is assimilated by a recognizable form. It is this fact that gives Shakespeare's work flesh and blood without sacrificing intellectual subtlety, and makes it universal in a way that certain forms of modern art, in spite of certain incidental values of great importance (particularly in cultural history), cannot attain by X-ray, infra-red, skeletal techniques.

We are in a better position to understand *Hamlet* as a great work once we are prepared for ambiguity and ambivalence presented according to impressionist techniques. We may be well acquainted with Shakespeare's ambivalence from other plays. Falstaff, for example, is ambivalent enough to provide a criticism of the morally correct as well as of the morally devious. Shylock, while in some ways ostensibly an anti-Semitic creation, provides a searching criticism of Christianity as in fact practised by Christians, and lays down a basic doctrine of common humanity.

Shakespeare's ambivalence rises from many factors. For one thing, it is deeply present in Christian traditions—in the paradox of the Pharisee and the Publican, of the first and the last, of saving one's life by losing it. It springs more immediately from an intense artistic objectivity; Shakespeare is never sentimental. Whatever may be the individual's situation or sufferings, the cosmic universe does not commit a pathetic fallacy to soothe him. Shakespeare is aware of irony in life as we know it—the world carries on, the sun shines, the rain falls, no matter how much personally one may suffer. The particular truth never quite fits with the convenient generalization; the good are not quite so good; the bad are not quite so bad. . . . "What a piece of work is a man" and "Imperial Caesar. . . . Might stop a hole to keep the wind away."

This ambivalence, of course, is the method by which Shakespeare's intellectual richness is expressed. But one should not infer that, because his thought is not neatly packaged, it lacks direction. On the contrary, this method adds the particular validity, arising from seeing experience on many levels at once, to a powerfully and logically motivated story, a story, in the case of *Hamlet*, of a particularly heroic figure. In AMERICA ("Hamlet a Hero in Two Senses," February 13, 1943) I placed particular emphasis on the need for recognizing the heroic element in Hamlet which has sometimes been obscured by other emphases. In that article I also suggested the value of understanding contemporary concepts of what constitutes a noble prince and ruler, an understanding that throws light on the ethical and juridical problem that Hamlet faces.

It is not my intention to repeat that content here. I would add, however, to those comments a further emphasis on the psychological aspects of the play. I think a distinction should be made between applying the important and sound discoveries of modern psychology and psychiatry to Shakespearean criticism and applying a kind of bumptious *patois* which, as in the field of social work, tends to classify persons as "types" and then to dismiss them as if all had been said that needed to be said. Hamlet may approach some "type"; he may be on the point of suffering from a definitely diagnosed type of mental disease. It is a tribute to Shakespeare's realism that his evidence can fit into a medical report; but what is more important, from the point of view of tragic conflict, is that Hamlet struggles with the difficulties that are threatening him with mental dissolution, and that at all times he remains a *human person* exercising the gravest moral responsibility under the gravest conditions.

I would not underrate the contributions of modern psychiatry in regard to a deeper knowledge of the human mind, especially on the experimental level. It is important to accept what is established in such sciences after critical winnowings. I believe that Freud has suffered from some of the same handicaps as did Darwin. Popularizers and an occasional loosely stated principle, or even an inaccurate principle, have overshadowed important and valuable research. Shakespeare touches upon certain inner tensions in *Hamlet* on which Freud has thrown light, but Shakespeare emphasizes, rather than threatens, moral responsibility.

T. S. Eliot in his *Collected Essays* rightly emphasizes the effect of Hamlet's relationship with his mother, though it is difficult to see how *Hamlet* may be considered an artistic failure because the problem cannot find an "objective equivalent" on the stage. Hamlet's deep underlying nausea, his hysteria which must increase in violence through the need for repression ("But break, my heart; for I must hold my tongue"), his melancholy, are more than usually clear in Shakespeare's ambiguous and ambivalent method. Shakespeare knew through experience that the conscious mind has a capacity for self-deception, that there are facts which for its own safety it attempts to forget or flee from; that men, too, are prompted at times by motives that they will not admit consciously to themselves.

For these reasons, examination of conscience and spiritual direction have always been important in the Catholic tradition. But just as a person who has suffered intense shock may not be fully aware of the repercussions of his experience, though a doctor or an outside observer would have no difficulties in seeing such causalities, so Hamlet becomes a subjective puzzle to himself and undoubtedly in our age would have profited from sound psychiatric help. Shakespeare, no less than Freud, though on a different level, was acquainted with the "rooted sorrow" of the mind. Shakespeare, it seems to me, is aware of what today we would call a mental "block" in Hamlet's admitted self-bafflement, which, it is to be noted, Hamlet attempts to overcome by seeking motivation:

> . . . Now, whether it be
> Bestial oblivion, or some craven scruple
> Of thinking too precisely on the event,
> A thought which, quarter'd, hath but one part wisdom
> And ever three parts coward, I do not know
> Why yet I live to say "This thing's to do";
> Sith I have cause and will and strength and means
> To do't.

To learn to know oneself, even when one comes to such an impasse, requires a desperate determination for integrity. Shakespeare is insistent in *Hamlet* that the difficulties a person meets on the intellectual and spiritual levels are complex and bewildering, that the road to wisdom cannot be run without humiliation and suffering.

For various historical reasons, particularly through the influence of Jansenism and Puritanism on moral values—with consequent too easy acceptance of the "fruits of sin" and of "bad blood"—and through the application by false analogy of mechanistic principles to the course of human life wherein everything is a matter of adjustment to environment, the average man has too many ready but inadequate answers for human experience. We strangely tend even to use our scientific knowledge to shield us from reality. Darwin is misapplied, and what is truly scientific in Freud is overlooked so that popularizations of thought attributed to these men may save us from the burden of moral responsibility But Shakespeare's *Hamlet* in some ways anticipates Freud without losing sight of the fact that our present existence is meaningful and decisive in regard to our eternal destiny—if we are the hollow men, we are the hollow men through our own choice. We cannot blame our stars, our atom bombs or our complexes.

Shakespeare never loses sight of the value of the objective order. He saw how objective evil can arise without corresponding moral responsibility. Ignorance, stupidity, self-deception shield the evildoer from adequate responsibility for his act, but the act has inevitable consequences in the objective order. A man is no less dead if he is killed with the best motives in the world, or with the worst, or with none at all. A moralist with a social conscience wishes to safeguard the objective order; he wishes to reduce the margin whereby objective evil may be done without the perpetrator realizing what he is doing; if he is a writer or a teacher he sees to it that no one goes unenlightened, if he can help it; for knowledge, though it makes the guilty guilty, helps to reduce what is objectively evil.

It is part of the irony omnipresent in Shakespeare and in life that Hamlet's mother, who is a stupid, shallow woman, almost neuter, is the immediate source of the evil that flows through the play, an evil the dimensions of which she is incapable of imagining. While Claudius had seen a choice and made it (his potentiality for evil was thereby limited), she needs the "glass" that Hamlet gives her so that she may see her inmost part. Shakespeare, aware of irony and the devastating effects of unconscious hypocrisy, stresses at all points moral responsibility—the course of life and of society runs according to decisions that are moral, not according to mechanistic or deterministic principles.

Moral responsibility in Shakespeare is not, however, just a burden. Implicit, for example, in *Hamlet* is the principle that Milton stated so often, that virtue alone is free. Hamlet suffers, it is true, through moral responsibility, but above all others in the play he can freely face and universalize the truth. He is free to transcend, to expand; he has the "bounty," the "franchise," the "magnanimity" that penetrates his personal crucifixion with the golden light of redemption and liberation. In this sense he is particularly the "noble heart."

Shakespeare is an important writer for an adult group; he can help us to attain adulthood, a life-long process. *Hamlet* particularly shocks what is timid and mediocre in us. National patterns of culture, which we cannot altogether escape, emphasize community respect, material comfort, "success," as the embracive and legitimate objects of human endeavor. If the gift of perpetual youth could only be added to these things, if death could only be exorcised, the design for living would be complete. Artistically, this picture of completeness can be obtained by simply ignoring all elements that conflict with, or deny, the wish fulfillments of mediocrity. In fact, this is the first principle a commercially successful writer learns. The basic cause for this mediocrity is the refusal to be adult—the refusal to face the facts of sin, pain and tragedy, and mystery.

But Shakespeare helps a little. He teaches us that there are only certain things about which we can be certain—that experience has many levels of mystery, some painful, which must be explored in each individual life. Chesterton once said that the object of the spiritual or artistic life was to "dig for the submerged sunrise of wonder"; but it is possible for us to become incapable of responding to reality simply because of the systematized social illusions which we accept from our environment. The following of *mores* is the mark of the grotesque child-adult, for whom life is a matter of the correct techniques or the right maneuvers, of saying the right thing at the right time; moral responsibility founded on growth and knowledge is the criterion of the adult.

WILLIAM J. GRACE

SELECTED BIBLIOGRAPHY

BRADLEY, A. C., *Shakespearean Tragedy*. Macmillan.
CAMPBELL, L. B., *Shakespeare's Tragic Heroes, Slaves of Passion*. Cambridge.
ELIOT, T. S., *Collected Essays*. Harcourt, Brace.
GRANVILLE-BARKER, H., *Prefaces to Shakespeare*. Third series. Princeton.
KNIGHT, G. W., *Wheel of Fire: Essays in Interpretation of Shakespeare's Somber Tragedies*. Oxford.
LEWIS, C. M., *The Genesis of Hamlet*. Holt.
SPENCER, Theodore, *Shakespeare and the Nature of Man*. Macmillan.
SPURGEON, C. E., *Shakespeare's Imagery*. Macmillan.
WILSON, J. D., *What Happens in Hamlet*. Macmillan.
CASTIGLIONE, B., *The Book of the Courtier*. Everyman's Library.
ELYOT, Thomas, *Boke Named the Governour*. Everyman's Library.
SHAKESPEARE, William, *Hamlet*. Random (Modern Library).

Locke: Of Civil Government

THE *Two Treatises of Civil Government,* of which the second is included in the Great Books program, was published by John Locke in 1690. Parliament had succeeded in ousting the last Stuart, James II, and in achieving its supremacy over the Crown in the "Glorious Revolution" of 1688. Locke sided with the Parliamentary party, the Whigs, for whom his Second Treatise became a political gospel.

The author of the *Two Treatises* lived a life of varied experiences at a critical period in English political history. He was born in 1632, found the Oxford lectures he had to attend pretty boring, but accepted a "senior studentship" in his college (Christ Church), an academic benefice of which Charles II deprived him in 1684. He turned his back on the ministry to study medicine, later serving as physician to Lord Ashley's household and tutor to that nobleman's grandson. Through his patron he entered upon a brief career of government service, followed by four years in France recovering his health. He then acted as adviser to Lord Shaftesbury and fell under a cloud as a consequence of his patron's conspiracy to dethrone Charles II.

In 1683 he took refuge in Holland, where he lived on the pension he enjoyed from Shaftesbury and on the income from the lands he inherited from his father. James II demanded his extradition. Although Locke was pardoned, he refused to return to England until after the accession of William of Orange, the choice of the victorious Parliamentary party.

He then became Commissioner of Appeals, a position providing him with an easy competence and a good deal of leisure for study, which he spent in Essex. He died in 1704.

No one has questioned Locke's sincerity. But he did build ideological fences around the interests of the landed aristocracy and the Parliamentary party whose favor he always enjoyed. As a result he has been for two and a half centuries an unseen lobbyist in every legislative meeting in English-speaking countries. The Lockian doctrine that the purpose of government is to protect the "natural rights" of private property and to leave the rest to "free enterprise" has been dressed up to give it the "new look" by labeling it "the American way." It has at one time or another captured control of both our major American political parties.

Locke, of course, wrote quite a few other important works, such as his *A Letter Concerning Toleration* and his philosophical treatise, the *Essay Concerning Human Understanding,* where he espoused a sensist psychology wholly at variance with his defense of the natural law in his political writings.

The second of the *Two Treatises of Civil Government* is worth reading more as a test of one's knowledge of political philosophy than as a piece of instruction.

For the most part, Locke did not originate the elements of his political thought. Taken one by one, they seem to echo traditional western and even Christian doctrines. But when Locke's thought takes on the proportions of a system, the reader will realize that he is confronted with a system at variance with that of Locke's scholastic predecessors.

The bias away from authentic Christian political thought really begins in the early chapters in a very unobtrusive way.

Catholic political philosophers had carefully chiseled out the two pillars on which the moral structure of the State rests. The first is the social nature of man, his moral obligation under the natural law to form a State and to cooperate with his fellow citizens in the promotion of the common good. Here man is not morally free. He is obliged (speaking generally) to enter into a political union. This is the first principle. It rests on man's intrinsic sociality.

But man is free to decide what kind of State he thinks will best achieve the individual and social purposes which the Creator has imbedded in our nature. All men being equal *as men,* no one has a right to exercise political authority over his fellows except through their consent. Hence arises the second principle of government based on consent, or popular sovereignty.

How does Locke handle these two starting principles? He begins with a lengthy disquisition on man in a "state of nature," with a view to setting forth man's "natural rights." He begins, as did the scholastics, with the divine natural law of morality. But how does he understand it? He puts all the stress on the natural "rights" man possesses before entering civil society. Is he or is he not upholding the intrinsic need of political society according to man's moral nature? This is the critical question the alert reader faces in the very first pages of the second *Treatise of Civil Government*. Locke opens Chapter VII by declaring:

> God, having made man such a creature that, in His own judgment, it was not good for him to be alone, put him under strong obligations of necessity, convenience and inclination to drive him into society, as well as fitted him with understanding and language to continue and enjoy it.

This sentence bears a very close resemblance to the scholastic doctrine of the intrinsically social nature of man. But does it really amount to an acceptance of the principle that membership in civil society is so intrinsically demanded by man's moral nature that life outside civil society must be termed "unnatural"? Or is Locke stopping short of that and making membership in civil society a matter of *convenience,* compelling as the reasons of convenience may be?

If Locke means what the scholastics mean, if the first interpretation is the right one, then why has he spent so much time elaborating his concept of human nature in terms of the state of nature? If "the state of nature" is (paradoxically) morally *unnatural* to man, what can we learn about his social and economic rights and duties by analyzing mankind in an unnatural condition?

But if Locke really means that political society is merely an expedient of convenience, a perfect arrangement by which the individual can shield, from the hazards of an unorganized multitude living in close proximity, the possessions he has acquired by "natural right," unrestrained by any social regulation, then his concern for what he supposes to be the individual's natural title to his property takes on a deep significance. This interpretation lines up Locke with the "rugged individualists" who look upon the State only as a means of protecting wealth acquired without any consideration for the well-being of the community. This, incidentally, is the concept of the State against which Karl Marx fired his heavy artillery. It is a target made to order for communist onslaughts, because it is morally indefensible.

As far as the essential propositions of political philosophy go, this is the one and only question to decide: is Locke an extreme individualist, a Spencerian before his time, or not? Is he just a "Liberty Leaguer," a laissez-fairist, an apostle of unlimited free enterprise? You can be sure of finding phrases in his treatise which seem to absolve him of this indictment. For consistency is a jewel conspicuously lacking in his crown. But he leans heavily to one side and must be classified where he falls. We often describe the laissez-faire system as one in which the State takes no sides, adopts no positive program to promote social justice and social welfare. Instead it stands outside the mêlee of free competition as an "umpire." Locke upheld this view and even employed the term "umpire" to describe it. A careful reader should be able to find the passage, for it is one of the most significant in the second Treatise.

One must also keep an eye out for the peculiar sense in which Locke uses the word "property." Does he consistently use it in this peculiar sense?

Locke undoubtedly defends the consent of the governed as the basis of political authority. But in his concept is this authority really *political?* To put the question differently, do citizens in Locke's state have a purpose essentially different from the purposes of the same individuals living in his "state of nature"?

The question may seem abrupt, but the real doubt to be cleared up in reading this classic is whether Locke's political society really has a specifically public purpose, at least in one economic sphere. If not, is it a State at all? That would be a strange State, which would ignore the means by which wealth was acquired and distributed and would intervene only to "freeze" the disorderly accumulations built up, as it were, behind its back. Its purpose would not be the public welfare, for it would be applying its police power to preserve the "take" of the "robber barons" of capitalism. It would be a State organized by one class to promote only the interests of that class.

In fairness to Locke one should recall that the viciousness of this theory was veiled until the industrial revolution hit its stride a full century after 1690. But what excuse can be offered in behalf of the millions of our contemporaries who still cling to this dishonored doctrine?

There are, to be sure, other interesting topics in Locke: his

concept of majority-rule, of checks and balances, of the ends of
government, of the role of legislative power (which he fences
round with strict limitations), of executive power, of the fiduciary
character of all political power, and of what he calls "prerogative"
(which he inflates in open contradiction to his theory of limited
government). What he has to say in his last chapter about the
"dissolution" of government or the right of revolution is especially interesting, if for no other reason than that the Declaration
of Independence could hardly have derived from Locke's roundabout handling of the issues uppermost in the minds of the
American colonists.

Locke is a strong exponent of the supremacy of law. As the
world is now divided into those who respect this ancient principle and those who make a mockery of it, his emphasis is timely.
Even his exposition of the natural right of private property, one-
sided as it is, contains some truths worth recalling in our day.
And his over-emphasis on free enterprise should not blind us to
the virtues of a system which, when properly regulated, is highly
productive and consistent with Christian social philosophy.

The trouble with Locke is that he identifies the right to one's
possessions with the absolute natural right to life itself. They
are not on a par. There seems to be no conventional scholastic
terminology to distinguish these two kinds of natural right. But
the right to life should be classified, in the opinion of the writer,
as a "perfectly constituted natural right." As soon as a human
being is conceived, whether in a "state of nature" or in civil
society, he has an absolute right to live. Even the State cannot
take the life of an innocent person. National self-defense may
require that he expose his life to danger, but it never requires
his death as a means to the self-preservation of society.

The right to private property, on the other hand, is an "imperfectly constituted natural right." One cannot define its extent
in a "state of nature" because one cannot determine in such a
mode of existence what limitations must be put upon property
rights in order to adjust them to the common welfare. Material
goods are subject to the temporal authority of the State in ways
in which the right to life, a spiritual good, is not. Why? Simply because material goods in themselves have a temporal purpose.
They are intended for the use of all men, and the right of private
property extends only as far as it provides the best means of

achieving the purpose of material goods. It is an essential means of achieving this purpose, but it offers no ultimate standard by which to insure that wealth be distributed in such wise that all men share in it according to a just proportion.

That standard is the common good, which includes the good of individuals as individuals and the good of individuals as members of society. Since no individual is competent to judge what demands the common welfare must make or may make upon private wealth, our human nature itself requires that we establish a public authority to decide and to enforce its decisions. That is surely one of the chief functions of the State, not merely to *protect* the possessions of individuals but to *promote* their common well-being by wise laws regulating the acquisition and use of property.

In such temporal concerns the individual, according to Thomistic political philosophy, is properly subordinated to the community. All modern States have been forced to throw overboard the Lockian theory because of the intolerable social injustice to which it inevitably led. Free societies have rejected Locke by peaceful means; unfree, by violent revolutions. Some, like the Communists, have gone much too far in the opposite direction. Others, like Britain and the western democracies of Europe, have adopted programs of nationalization of key-industries in an attempt to restore order to societies ravaged first by industrial capitalism and then by war.

The United States is trying to find a stable equilibrium between various forms of governmental control and regulation, on the one side, and free enterprise on the other. No nation has yet found a satisfactory solution to the problem of harnessing industrial capitalism to the social ends an economic system ought to serve. The problem embraces two fields: one, that of social and political philosophy, wherein citizens, not only within each nation but throughout the world, can come to an agreement about the ends they need to work for conjointly; the other, that of social, political, and economic institutions by which to achieve those agreed-upon ends.

Each of these two problems is discouragingly complex at best, and has been made indescribably more complex by the disruptions of war and the cleavage of peoples into democratic and Communist camps. It is safe to say that as the problems took centuries to unfold, the solutions will require centuries to build up. Like the medieval cathedrals, these constructive remedies will, if achieved, incorporate the contributions of successive generations of devoted believers in the moral nobility of mankind. Every serious reader of Locke can feel that he is helping to clear away the debris, as men are doing in Europe, and trying to salvage from the past whatever wisdom has stood the test of time and can be used to buttress and rebuild the sagging arches of our social, economic, and political edifices.

ROBERT C. HARTNETT

SELECTED BIBLIOGRAPHY

JONES, W. T., *Masters of Political Thought*. Vol. II, Machiavelli to Bentham. Houghton Mifflin.

KENDALL, Willmoore, *John Locke and the Doctrine of Majority Rule*. Urbana: University of Illinois Press.

LOCKE, John, *Of Civil Government*. Dutton. (Everyman's Library Edition).

SABINE, George H., *A History of Political Theory*. Holt.

Rousseau: The Social Contract

As MONTAIGNE is the first, Rousseau is the second great witness to the disintegration of Western thought since the Reformation and the Renaissance. Western thought reached its highest integration with St. Thomas and St. Bonaventure, who utilized the best pagan thought and made the full weight of Christian Revelation bear on the problems of the nature of ultimate reality, of the nature of man, of his consequent inalienable rights, and of his relations to God and his fellowmen, including government. Montaigne lived in the turmoil of the Protestant Revolt. The *magisterium* of Revelation was already sapped by private judgment. Renaissance scholarship and printing had brought back all pre-Christian thought. Montaigne is the first bewildered modern. In his study he oscillates between Christianity—which he still understands—Stoic pride, skepticism and Epicurean relaxation.

The seventeenth century labored at a Christian reaction, but it failed. The generation of Louis XIV saw the triumph of neo-paganism to an extent often not understood. It compromised Catholicism, developed a social life subtly erotic, functioned to the advantage of a parasitic aristocracy artificially extravagant, under a Roman-law-inspired absolute monarchy which absorbed churchmen and found in them apologists.

The result was the upheaval of the eighteenth century. Voltaire, the high Parisian bourgeois, behind "the Enlightenment" lashed at the Church and Christianity as the foes of hedonistic material progress; Rousseau, the Genevan plebeian, exalted the people and, to ensure virtue to society, finally oriented it toward totalitarianism. As Goethe said: "With Voltaire, the old order died, with Rousseau, the new began. . . ."

A good case can be made for the unity of Rousseau's life's work. Born in 1712, he came out of obscurity in Paris in 1750 by winning a Dijon Academy prize for an essay on: "Did the

development of the sciences and arts help to improve morals?"
No, answered Rousseau, they are born of, and feed on, our vices,
and stress the fatal inequality of talents. To burn all books, save
the Gospels, would be a service, for books help change the good
and simple natural man to the artificial social man. Should we
then go back to the savage state? Impossible. Let then the sciences
and arts at least soften the ferocity of those they have corrupted.

Rousseau was his own first convert. He broke with the circles
he had courted, stressed his Swiss republicanism, lived with a
simple servant he had married, copied music for a living, refused
to be presented to the King after having inconsistently written a
successful opera, went back to Geneva and Calvinism which he
had, as a youth, abjured for Catholicism, after running away from
home. In 1755, the Dijon Academy proposed another subject:
"The Origin and Foundation of Inequality among Men."
Rousseau answered: Property. In the state of nature men were
happy but, when they enclosed land, rivalries began. Then the
richer, stronger, more intelligent joined against the poor and
weak, and inequalities were consecrated by time and maintained
by force.

Back in Paris new friends protected him in spite of his constant rudeness. Mme. d'Epinay gave him an hermitage on her
Montmorency estate near Paris. There (1756-57) he ripened his
theories, fell in love with his protectress' sister, was dismissed,
took refuge in the village, wrote a letter to d'Alembert on the
theatre—a new occasion to condemn the arts: tragedy flatters
dangerous passions and comedy derides virtue. Then the Lord of
Montmorency took him into his own household, and there
Rousseau brought out his three great works in 1761 and 1762:
New Héloise, which preached the reform of the family and of
social life; *Emile,* the reform of the individual through education; *The Social Contract,* the reform of the State.

Thus was his work consistently completed. After that came
"persecutions." The Parliament condemned *Emile* and wanted
to imprison the author. Rousseau fled to Switzerland, and from
there wrote a long letter to M. de Beaumont, archbishop of Paris,
who had likewise condemned the book. But the Consistory of
Geneva also denounced him, whereupon he left Switzerland to
wander in France till he took refuge with Hume in England,
only to quarrel with him. Back in Paris in 1770, he lived feeling

haunted but still looked after, finished his *Confessions*, wrote his romantic *Reveries of a Solitary Wanderer,* and died of a stroke in 1778 in the home of a last protector at Ermenonville, near Paris. Buried on the estate, his remains were placed in 1794 near those of Voltaire in the Pantheon, the disaffected church on the site of the Paris Abbey built by Clovis and St. Genevieve, and now consecrated to the saints of the Republic. His main works were naturally put on the *Index:* the *Emile* in 1762, the *Contrat Social* and the *Lettre à M. de Beaumont* in 1766, though *Nouvelle Héloise* was not listed there till 1806.

No man has been more violently denounced than Rousseau. Maritain sums it up: "A prodigious perverter who gave us that cadaver of Christian ideas the immense putrefaction of which now poisons the world." No doubt, but nevertheless far from the whole picture. Rousseau was often declamatory, but he weaned literature from the abstract dryness of decadent classicism, and made sentences throb with music as never before. He over-sentimentalized nature, but he taught us to see it and feel its mystery. His *Confessions* are often bombastic and shameless, but he re-opened the whole field of personal literature. His denunciations of the arts and sciences and of the theatre are extreme, but so are Bossuet's, and only virulent attacks could challenge the pride of the day.

His *New Heloise* may be in spots a perverting school of romantic love, but the life of the common man is opposed to the artificialities of the aristocratic circles, the beauties of nature again abundantly revealed, while the often ridiculous sentimentality which runs through the whole is at least superior to the cynical eroticism of the day. *Emile,* particularly, is full of fallacies, impractical, as Rousseau himself recognized; and it is always retold how he put his own five children in a foundlings' home. He was nevertheless right in calling for a more natural education of children, for less coercing, punishing, rewarding, for teaching through experience and the utilization of the child's natural interest, and for the awakening of the child's initiative and creativeness through internal motivation.

Rousseau may have distorted many Christian virtues, but at least he attacked many un-Christian and unnatural abuses. He cannot be repudiated wholesale without repudiating most of what we are glad to have become—a democracy, for example, communities living a simple even if gadgeted life, parents living in comradeship with their children. He was the champion of the common man when even American colonists despised him. It is more profitable to study Rousseau objectively to learn the secret of his imaginative and emotional expression, and especially to understand how his inconsistencies and his contradictions were those of his age. If he misused Christian thought, it was largely because he found it already disintegrated. We need to study his very failures if we would ourselves achieve its reintegration.

Albert Schinz, in his *La Pensée de Jean-Jacques Rousseau* (Alcan, 1929), gave us the most data for that study. Against the undiscriminating denouncers of Rousseau as an anarchistic romantic, he shows that Rousseau was really constantly torn between his romantic trust in the goodness of nature, a reaction from his Calvinism, and a Roman or stoic streak stemming both from his Calvinism and his early reading of Plutarch. In short, as in Montaigne, as Victor Hugo will say of himself, there were two men in him—he represented the modern man's perpetual conflict between the drive of a would-be-emancipated ego toward liberty and license and the awareness of the need of some discipline.

So, as Schinz points out, in his first discourse Rousseau extols Roman virtue, and in the second he shifts to the exaltation of the supposed original goodness—or at least lack of perversion—of primitive peoples. He has now rejected the Calvinistic doctrine that man is naturally bad, and seeks a basis for human happiness through virtue. In *New Héloise* he complacently describes romantic love, but he works out a stoic social morality which would save his heroine. In *Emile,* his final and greatest effort to systematize his thought, he would procure the child's happiness through the use of his natural interests in the development of his powers; but when he comes to the need of giving him a moral code, he first tries disinterestedness, realizes its inadequacy, and concludes with the need of religion. Hence the final profession of faith of the Vicaire Savoyard, and his exaltation of conscience: "I see God everywhere in His works and I feel Him within me."

It is against this whole background that *The Social Contract* should be studied. It raises the final question of the securing of individual and social happiness through order: how far is government necessary and what should it be to secure these ends?

Schinz shows that it is in this work that Rousseau's contradictory tendencies culminate, from its opening sentence: "Man is born free and everywhere is in chains," to the final chapter in which to secure man's freedom Rousseau hands him over, bound soul and body, to the totalitarian state.

The problem haunted him even before 1754, as shown in an *Encyclopédie* article on "Political Economy." In that article "the general will" and not "the social contract" is for him its first principle. But he reflects: What will make the individual man sacrifice his particular will to the general will, and what will insure the justice of magistrates? He now forgets so completely his doctrine of the natural goodness of man that he leaves the question unanswered. It is only after 1757, when he returns to the subject, that he finally brings in the idea of the social contract as a possible basis for ensuring the enforcement of the law. ·

This idea was of course not original with him, since it had been utilized by La Boétie and Hooker in the sixteenth century, by Grotius, Milton, Hobbes and Locke in the seventeenth; and, in fact, goes back to the Epicureans of antiquity, who held that justice was based on a social compact entered into by primitive men in self-defense and for self-preservation. So Rousseau's original subject appears in the subtitle of what he now calls: *The Social Contract, or Principles of Political Law.*

His first draft shows that his new approach still leaves him perplexed. He ventures: "Let all surrender their will, their goods, their person, under the contract to the general will," with the implication that each one will then obey only himself indirectly and thus retain his freedom. But that is not answering the question: will the law be obeyed against self-interest? Rousseau then reasons: "In order that the Social Contract be not a vain formula, the state, independently of the consent of the citizens, must have some guarantee of their obeying the law. Citizens must be made to swear to uphold it." Even then the oath must have a sanction. So Rousseau is led to write: "The fundamental pact implies tacitly this engagement which alone can guarantee all the others, that whoever refuses to obey the general will will be compelled to by the whole body."

But the contradictions still stand. As Schinz recalls, Rousseau in his first draft had a second chapter: "The General Society of Human Kind," in which he recognized that men will not observe, without being forced to do so, any clause of the contract working to their disadvantage, and a third chapter, "The Fundamental Pact," in which he pretends that they will spontaneously observe the contract in all circumstances. He had to choose between them. Hurried by his printer, he did so by suppressing the second. Later he would write: "As for *The Social Contract,* those who will pretend to understand it entirely are smarter than I am. It needs to be rewritten, but I have no longer the strength nor the time to do so."

This means that the readers of the final draft of Books I and II should not be surprised if they find in them contradictions. It also means that, inconsistently with his romantic trust in human nature but consistently with his realism, Rousseau was finally led to say not only that citizens must be coerced to obey the law, but that the law must have a religious sanction. Rousseau's final position is then that the State cannot subsist unless the citizens have religious beliefs which will motivate them from within to obey even against self-interest.

Thus did Rousseau come to formulate his "civil religion" in Book IV, chapter eight, and that chapter must be read because that is the chapter which shows how Rousseau became a fountain-head of totalitarianism:

There is then a purely civil profession of faith, of which the sovereign must fix the articles, not as religious dogmas, but as social sentiments without which it is impossible to be a faithful citizen or subject. . . . The positive dogmas of this civil religion are: The existence of a divinity, powerful, intelligent, good, foreseeing and providing; an afterlife, the reward of the good, the punishment of the wicked and the sanctity of contracts and laws.

Rousseau at last had the needed sanction both for the law and the contract, but he left it to the State to formulate it and to enforce it, and to a State before which the individual had no longer any inalienable rights: "The State has the duty to banish anyone who cannot accept these dogmas, and to put to death anyone who, having publicly recognized them, acts against them. He has committed the greatest of crimes, he lied before the law." And again: "When the sovereign says: It is expedient that you die, the citizen must die, since his life is not only a gift of nature but a conditional gift of the state."

Rousseau's entire work is completely expressive of the dislocated thought of his time and the consequent conflict in his own mind. Rousseau must be granted a genuine moral earnestness. He was deeply conscious of the consequences of the ethos of his day—its sexual laxity, its artificial life, the neo-paganism in its art and literature, its social injustices—and the general failure, exhibited in his own life, to solve the problem of the necessary discipline of the natural man better than Calvinism allowed, but, as he saw him, corrupted by civilization.

St. Paul had expressed the problem once for all and pointed out the remedy: grace through Jesus Christ. But in Rousseau's day the Church and the sects had long been at odds over grace and its means; Christ was repudiated by the Deists, God by the materialists, and Rousseau himself saw in Christianity an anti-social force, since it "made men indifferent to their own temporal good and to the good of the state." Out of this disintegration he would at least rescue the thought of God, but he did so only to turn God over to Caesar.

So Rousseau helped to break the link that bound the political rights of man to his God-given nature; and the Christian Church with her divine foundation. He should then be studied as a witness to the disintegration of Western thought in his own age, and as a contributor to its even greater disintegration in ours, which has left even his Deism behind and believes only, as some of the later Great Books will show, in the evolution of a self-existing universe in search of an ever new pragmatic morality over which now looms the specter of a world-throttling absolute state.

Louis J. A. Mercier

SELECTED BIBLIOGRAPHY

Babbitt, Irving, *Rousseau and Romanticism.* Houghton Mifflin.
Maritain, Jacques, *Three Reformers.* Scribner.
Rousseau, Jean-Jacques, *The Social Contrast.* Random (Modern Library).
Masson, P. M., *La Religion de J. J. Rousseau.* Hachett.
Seillière, E., *J. J. Rousseau.* Garnier.
Annales de la Société J. J. Rousseau. Champion.

Federalist Papers

OF THE eighty-five papers in the complete text of *The Federalist,* the booklet issued by the Great Books Foundation includes only eighteen. For some reason the first ten essays are reproduced, with only eight of the remaining seventy-five. Complete editions are easy enough to lay hold of, however, and the specimens made available to students of the Great Books are well enough chosen to bring readers into that intimacy with great thinkers for which the program was designed.

The Federalist is probably one of the most frequently mentioned but least-read volumes in the literature of the world. When the essays first appeared, a French diplomatic official took a very sophisticated view of them. "This work," he wrote home, "is of no use to educated persons, and is too learned for the uneducated." In his judgment, *The Federalist* fell between two stools and was therefore a literary "flop." What "flopped" was rather his literary judgment. For from the start the essays won the respect of the learned. Jefferson wrote to his friend Madison from Paris on November 18, 1788, that *The Federalist* was "in my opinion, the best commentary on the principles of government which ever was written." On March 4, 1825, in a report of the Board of Visitors of the University of Virginia, he was at pains to declare where the principles of government to be inculcated in the University could be found. After mentioning The Declaration of Independence, Jefferson wrote:

The book known by the title of "The Federalist," being an authority to which appeal is habitually made by all, and rarely declined or denied by any as evidence of the general opinion of those who framed, and of those who accepted the Constitution of the United States, on questions as to its genuine meaning.

It is characteristic of the Sage of Monticello that he next included the Virginia Resolutions of 1799, which flatly contradicted the constitutional doctrine of the authority of the Supreme Court as set forth in *The Federalist.*

The Federalist has, indeed, achieved the highest distinction attainable by a work on political science in this country. It has frequently been cited by the Supreme Court itself as evidence of "the genuine meaning" of disputed provisions in the Constitution. It has become what jurists call "a source of law."

The Constitutional Convention agreed upon the Constitution in September, 1787. The plan itself had carefully provided that ratification should take place, not through State legislatures, but through conventions of nine States.

The State legislatures were by-passed in favor of popular ratification for two reasons. On the constitutional side, the State legislatures themselves enjoyed only limited and delegated authority. It was more than doubtful that they possessed the juridical authority to re-delegate their powers to a new national government. Madison and James Wilson, joined by Gouverneur Morris, Col. George Mason, Rufus King and others, had fought right up to the end in the Constitutional Convention to have the Constitution submitted to *the people of the States* for ratification, rather than to State legislatures, because they did not want the new Union to be founded as a mere *league of States.* The States' Rights delegates opposed this procedure, but the group later called Federalists won the day for ratification by the people of the States instead of by State legislatures. It was a momentous victory: a national State was born out of it.

Besides the constitutional reason for popular ratification, there were political reasons. The framers knew full well that the State officials entrenched in power would be the last voluntarily to dismantle the political mansions in which they dwelt in splendor.

Hamilton estimated that sentiment in New York State, where the anti-Federalist party of Governor George Clinton was in control, was about two to one against ratification. He invited Madison and John Jay to collaborate with him in publishing a series of articles in the public press to explain and defend the Constitution. The eighty-five articles appeared under the pseudonym of "Publius" from October, 1787, a few weeks after the close of the Philadelphia Convention, to May, 1788, a few weeks before the opening of the New York State ratifying convention at Poughkeepsie.

The authorship of Nos. 18-20, 49-58 and 62-63 (fifteen papers) has long been in dispute. Editions of *The Federalist* commonly assign them to "Hamilton or Madison." Douglass Adair in *The William and Mary Quarterly* for April and July, 1944, has pretty well proved Madison's authorship of these papers.

What success did *The Federalist* papers have in bringing New York into the fold? It is hard to say. Hamilton used and improved the arguments therein set forth in his one-man battle for ratification at Poughkeepsie. He won: 30-27. Melancthon Smith, his only formidable opponent, himself capitulated. But it was Hamilton's threat to separate the southern counties of New York and bring them into the Union without the rest of the State that broke the back of the opposition.

The leading characteristic of *The Federalist's* argument is its concept of the basic problem of government. Both Hamilton (in No. 1) and Madison (in No. 37) envisage it as "combining the requisite of stability and energy in government, with the inviolable attention due to liberty and to the republican form." Jefferson, on the other hand, showed little concern for the requisite of strength. His vocabulary is full of terms like "liberty," "freedom," "oppression," "tyranny," as if political society could be held together by the loose bond of a common desire for independence of governmental restraints.

It is with Madison's famous paper on the inevitability of factions (No. 10) that *The Federalist* begins to sound the depths of political philosophy. Political liberty, in Madison's philosophy, naturally opens the door to class antagonisms. Indeed, the only guarantee of liberty is that interest-groups are multiplied to a point where no one commands a majority. His slogan was "to enlarge the sphere as far as the nature of the government would admit," so that by introducing more and more forms of division, the danger of a unified majority, capable of oppressing a minority, would be neutralized. This principle he had expounded on the floor of the Constitutional Convention on June 6.

One might well ask whether this principle conforms to the genuine concept of the common good as embodied in traditional Christian political philosophy. Whence did Madison derive this idea?

This same idea is set forth in essay No. 51, which deals with the subject of checks and balances. Does it not offer internal evidence of Madison's authorship of this disputed paper?

For this is one topic on which we find Hamilton and Madison in open discord. Although Hamilton's papers Nos. 35 and 36 clearly suggest his opposition to Madison's views on factions, we must turn to his unparalleled speech on the Senate in the Poughkeepsie convention for the complete contradiction:

Much has been said about factions. . . . We are attempting by this Constitution to abolish factions, and to unite all parties for the general welfare [quoted in *Hamiltonian Principles,* ed. James Truslow Adams, p. 11].

Hamilton certainly did not believe that liberty inevitably gave birth to factions, and that it owed its continued existence to the neutralizing effect of factions upon one another. Who is the optimist and who the pessimist in this division of opinion?

Paper No. 15, by Hamilton, has a great contemporary interest. It is enough to ask whether the Charter of the United Nations recognizes what Hamilton calls "the great and radical vice" in the structure of the Articles of Confederation which preceded our Constitution. This is the attempt to *legislate for States or governments in their collective capacities,* instead of legislating for the individuals who compose them.

When we read essay No. 31, by Hamilton, we feel a marked change of intellectual atmosphere. A Thomist senses straight off that he is at home with a mind trained to think in terms of first principles:

In disquisitions of every kind there are certain primary truths, or first principles, upon which all subsequent reasonings must depend. These contain an internal evidence which, antecedent to all reflections or combinations, commands the assent of the mind.

Is not Hamilton's manner of defending the new Constitution noticeably different from Madison's? If so, in what does the difference consist?

Madison was a capable political thinker, as his handling of the question of the principle of separation of powers in No. 47 amply shows. But for carrying a set of principles through one phase of government after the other, as Hamilton did in his papers on the national Executive (Nos. 68-71 in the Great Books edition), is he comparable with the great New Yorker?

If one wishes to read further in this classic volume, where should one turn?

Madison's essay on the question whether the new Constitution really would establish a *republic* of a truly *federal* type (No. 39) is worth studying for the definition of these terms. Westbrook Pegler and others like to distinguish between present trends in popular control of American Government and the "republican" type intended by the Founding Fathers. Does this essay substantiate their contention?

In view of the later conflict between Hamilton on the one side and Jefferson and Madison on the other over the scope of national powers, papers Nos. 41, 44 and 45, by Madison, are illuminating. So is his next paper, in which he proposes the very sensible argument that the *people* of the United States should be left to decide whether they wish to have this or that function performed by their State or their National Governments.

Characteristic papers by Hamilton are Nos. 23 and 28, in which he expresses his belief in wide national powers; No. 25, in which he foresaw the need of unlimited means of national self-defense; No. 30, in which he defended the Federal taxing power —a topic of ever-current interest; and No. 33, in which he expounded his famous conception of "implied powers." Madison treated the same topic in No. 44, an example of the repetitiousness of *The Federalist,* but one which raises the question of why Madison later opposed Hamilton on this doctrine.

Readers who have a special interest in the Federal Judiciary will find Hamilton's famous papers from No. 78 onward a delight. The first Secretary of the Treasury is not well known as a great constitutional lawyer, but do not these essays rank with the decisions of John Marshall as landmarks of early American constitutional thought?

No classic of human thought yields its riches without serious intellectual work on the part of the reader. Whoever expects every page to intrigue him is expecting more than human genius has produced. The classics live because they reach heights unreached by the general run of literary works. *The Federalist* ascends as many peaks as any of them. The day Americans find it too much trouble to study, they will forfeit democracy.

ROBERT C. HARTNETT

SELECTED BIBLIOGRAPHY

ADAIR, Douglass, "The Authorship of the Disputed Federalist Papers," *The William and Mary Quarterly*, Third Series, I (April and June, 1944) 97-122, 235-264.

ADAMS, Randolph (ed.), *Hamiltonian Principles: Extracts from the Writings of Alexander Hamilton*. Little, Brown.

BRANT, Irving, *James Madison: The Nationalist 1780-1787*. Bobbs-Merrill.

HAMILTON, Alexander, Madison, James, and Jay, John, *The Federalist*. Random (Modern Library).

OLIVER, Frederick Scott, *Alexander Hamilton: An Essay on American Union*. London: Archibald Constable.

Adam Smith: The Wealth of Nations

The Wealth of Nations is "secular in tone, rationalist in method, and individualist in outlook." This from the pen of the contemporary British political scientist and pamphleteer, Mr. Harold Laski, who himself is almost the perfect paradigm of the first and second, though not the third, of the adjectives which he uses to describe so accurately the masterpiece of one of the most illustrious names that are to be found in the history of economic thought.

Laski's emphasis, it will be noted, is on the social and political philosophy of Adam Smith and only indirectly, if at all, on his economics—an emphasis which is not altogether improper in analyzing a treatise now known to have been an elaboration of an earlier course in ethics (*Theory of Moral Sentiments*) delivered by Dr. Smith in the 1750's at the University of Glasgow. "Adam Smith's great work," says an American writer, John M. Ferguson,

... was much more than its title would lead one to believe. It was not only a treatise on economics, dealing in a many-sided fashion with the wealth of nations, but a comprehensive philosophical work, treating in a broad way of problems of human welfare. Economic principles, ethical principles, principles of jurisprudence, principles of theology—all these pass in review before the reader in this book of nearly nine hundred pages.

"Much more than its title would lead one to believe"— and much more, of course, than a reading of the first nine chapters of Book I would lead one to suspect. It is for this reason, among others, that the present summary will necessarily make reference, at least in passing, to phases of Smith's philosophy which are not always explicitly expounded in those first nine chapters of *The Wealth of Nations* to which the Great Books course presumably is limiting its attention. It might even be suggested, incidentally, that the participants in the course will be wasting their time if they limit themselves too scrupulously to their formal assignment. Or is it possible to understand *The Wealth of Nations* by reading a section of Book I, when, as even a casual glance at the index will indicate, it isn't until Book IV that the author gets around to developing his celebrated theory of the "invisible hand" and his theory on the limited role of government?

Suffice it to say that Smith's historical influence—and it has been tremendous, even though sometimes in directions which he himself might have repudiated—stems predominantly from the fact that, in the words of Max Lerner, "he gave a new dignity to greed and a new sanctification to the predatory impulses." Or, again in the language of Laski: "With Adam Smith the practical maxims of business enterprise achieved the status of a theology; and the state became the instrument by which, in the next seventy years, they were applied to the practice of its daily life." These things Smith did principally in Book IV, it is suggested, and only incidentally (at least less emphatically) in the early chapters of Book I.

The Wealth of Nations was first and foremost an indictment of and a brilliant protest against the confining governmental restrictions and controls of the system of economic mercantilism in which the author's own generation was entangled and against which it was already protesting—overtly at times, but more often by smuggling and by a "tacit acquiescence on the part of many legislators in the breakdown of a policy to which theoretical allegiance was still the rule throughout the country" (Ferguson). Eighteenth-century England, then, and particularly eighteenth-century business men, were psychologically very receptive to Smith's apotheosis of the individual and his corresponding indictment of governmental intervention in economic affairs.

Smith's conclusions about the sanctity of individual liberty— fittingly enough for one who had once been a professor of ethics —were based on certain theoretical assumptions about the nature of man. Human conduct, according to Smith (the philosopher speaking, not the economist), is naturally activated by six motives: self-love, sympathy, the desire to be free, a sense of propriety, a habit of labor, and the propensity to truck, barter and exchange one thing for another. On the basis of these six assumptions, he argued that each man is *naturally* (i.e. by the law of nature) the best judge of his own economic welfare and that, marvelous to relate, in pursuing his own individual welfare without let or hindrance he would thereby automatically and inevitably (again by the law of nature) be promoting the common good as well.

It was the latter conclusion, of course, which was welcomed so enthusiastically by contemporary enterprisers. And why not? Why not, indeed—for it assured them, in terms of a natural and immutable law, that far from being enemies of the general welfare in pursuing their own unlimited profit, in reality they were to be blessed as public benefactors. "Every individual," says Smith,

is continually exerting himself to find out the most advantageous employment for whatever capital he can command. It is his own advantage, indeed, and not that of the society, which he has in view. But the study of his own advantage naturally, or rather necessarily, leads him to prefer that employment which is most advantageous to the society. . . . He generally, indeed, neither intends to promote the public interest, nor knows how much he is promoting it. By preferring the support of domestic to that of foreign industry, he intends only his own security; . . . he intends only to his own gain, and he is in this, as in many other cases, *led by an invisible hand* to promote an end which was no part of his intention. (Italics added)

Comforting words, to be sure, not alone to Smith's contemporaries, but to far too many of us today, who, to our shame, neglect the tons of evidence which are in front of us to demonstrate the fallacy of Smith's philosophy of economic life.

Corollary to the "invisible hand" theory (which, in reality, as even unbelievers must admit, is a vulgar, though well-intentioned, parody on the doctrine of Providence) is Smith's rejection of governmental intervention in the affairs of economic life. The pertinent reference from *The Wealth of Nations* is (unfortunately) so much a part of our culture that one almost apologizes for quoting it again:

Every man, as long as he does not violate the laws of justice, is left perfectly free to pursue his own interest his own way, and to bring forth his industry and capital into competition with those of any other man, or order of men. The sovereign is completely discharged from a duty, in the attempting to perform which he must always be exposed to innumerable decisions, and for the proper performance of which no human wisdom or knowledge could ever be sufficient; the duty of superintending the industry of private people, and of directing it towards the employments most suitable to the interest of the society.

According to the system of natural liberty, the sovereign has only three duties to attend to . . . : first, the duty of protecting the society from the violence and invasion of other independent societies; secondly, the duty of protecting, as far as possible, every member of the society from the injustice or oppression of every other member of it . . . ; and, thirdly, the duty of erecting and maintaining certain public works and institutions, which it can never be for the interest of any individual, or small number of individuals, to erect and maintain.

"Anarchy plus a constable," in the language of Carlyle!

Be it said in Smith's defense that he was under no illusions about the altruism of business men. Far from underestimating the selfishness of human beings, he accepts it as the basis of his reasoning. In fact, as we have already indicated, he openly glorifies it as the catalyst of economic progress. But how shall society protect itself against the extortionate practices of the wealthy and the powerful?

The question, of course, is irrelevant. Competition (competition unlimited either by the government or by the self-discipline of guilds or similar associations) is the only protection that society needs and the only protection that nature (read: Adam Smith) will countenance. Automatic control of industry through competitive prices, he believed, would force the business man, in his own interest, to produce and to trade in those commodities which the people wanted and would thus actually hand over the final control of production and commerce to consumers. Smith was realistic enough, of course, to have his misgivings about the beneficence of competition in its treatment of the unprotected worker, but not sufficiently realistic to have serious doubts about the absolute validity of the principle of competition as such.

Adam Smith undoubtedly looked upon himself as a social reformer, and in all fairness it ought to be said that in many respects he was. Scattered throughout his masterpiece are references to the workers, which, by contrast with certain subsequent theories and public policies, are eminently decent and humane. Smith was interested in one objective only—to blast away the crippling restrictions of mercantilism, to open the door to freedom, and thus, as he imagined, to increase the wealth of nations and of peoples. Perhaps it is unwarrantedly harsh to refer to him, as Lerner does, as "an unconscious mercenary in the service of a rising capitalist class in Europe." Perhaps. But this much is true, and tragically so, that history (with infallibly perfect logic, of course) has used his classical rationalization of human greed as a sanctimonious camouflage for ghastly economic oppression and tyranny. His heritage to later generations—although obviously he alone was not responsible—has been described by Pope Leo XIII as follows:

> After the old trade guilds had been destroyed in the last century, and no protection was substituted in their place, and when public institutions and legislation had cast off traditional religious teaching, it gradually came about that the present age handed over the workers, each alone and defenseless, to the inhumanity of employers and the unbridled greed of competitors. A devouring usury, although often condemned by the Church, but practised nevertheless under another form by avaricious and grasping men, has increased the evil; and in addition the whole process of production as well as trade in every kind of goods has been brought almost entirely under the power of a few, so that a very few rich and exceedingly rich men have laid a yoke almost of slavery on the unnumbered masses of non-owning workers.

That Smith himself, had he lived through the nineteenth century and were he alive today, might have repudiated the uncritical application of his principles to a totally different set of economic circumstances has often been suggested.

Let us concede that the suggestion is warranted. Let us concede, in other words, that Smith's native honesty would have compelled him to admit, as many of his latter-day disciples have refused to admit, that the Industrial Revolution has so radically and completely transformed our economic institutions that competition, as he understood the concept, simply doesn't exist today in large areas of our economic life. It is comforting and permissible to imagine that he would be the first to ridicule some of the hokum of the National Association of Manufacturers—to single out one of the worst among contemporary offenders—in pretending that there is anything more than a verbal resemblance between the "competition" of *The Wealth of Nations* and the numerous types of monopoly and monopolistic competition which the publicity experts of the NAM consistently try to palm off on a much too gullible public.

Granted, however, that Smith was personally honest and sincere, what can history conclude about his principal theories as

such? Only that they were fallacious and inherently so—prescind-
ing, that is, from the fact that they have worked out very badly
in practice. In denying the social nature of man, he canonized
a type of economic individualism which is (or ought to be) as
repugnant to the Christian as the opposite evil of collectivism—
which, incidentally, owes almost as much to Adam Smith for
its current successes as it does to Marx himself.

Father Gerald Walsh, S.J., of Fordham University, in his recent
booklet entitled *Catholicism,* reminds us sagely that

the deepest source of the nostalgia, of the homesickness, for [religious]
faith is, I think, to be found in the character of modern economic
life and in the present direction of international affairs. The political
economy of Adam Smith has given us no answer to the cruelties of
social injustice, nor is the jurisprudence of Bentham any solution to
the political absurdities of the omnipotent state. It was inevitable,
therefore, that the claim of religion to put a curb on absolute ownership and absolute sovereignty should awaken curiosity in the world
today concerning the conception of that unique Omnipotence whose
name is God.

This sense of religious curiosity, so providentially emerging out
of the depths of disillusionment and despair, can develop, under
God, into an attitude of scientific inquiry. If it does, it will discover in the social teaching of the Church a body of principles
which explicitly contradict the basic social philosophy of Adam
Smith and which, if implemented without unnecessary delay, can
wipe out the blight of economic secularism which the well-intentioned Glasgow moralist has bequeathed, let us hope un-
wittingly, to the twentieth century—a century in which the social
nature of man, however tragically and irrationally, is wreaking
its vengeance in purges, in concentration camps and in wars and
rumors of wars.

GEORGE C. HIGGINS

SELECTED BIBLIOGRAPHY

HUGHES, Emmett, *The Church and the Liberal Society.* Princeton.
ROLL, Eric, *A History of Economic Thought.* Prentice-Hall.
LASKI, Harold, *The Rise of Liberalism.* Harper.
WHITTAKER, Edmund, *A History of Economic Ideas.* Longmans, Green.
FERGUSON, John M., *Landmark in Economic Thought.* Longmans, Green.
NORTHRUP, F. S. C., *The Meeting of East and West.* Macmillan.
ROYAN, John A., *A Better Economic Order.* Harper.
SMITH, Adam, *The Wealth of Nations.* Random (Modern Library).

Karl Marx: Communist Manifesto

IF A GREAT book is one that has dominated innumerable minds and launched a grand-style social movement, then this is one of the greatest. Through it was organized into a mighty social force the socialist movement which, before its publication, had existed among only a few tiny and unrelated groups of intellectuals. Its words inspired some of the leaders of the Russian branch of the movement to seize power in the name of communism. He who wants fully to understand the tragic conflict of our day, which makes peace precarious and the survival of Western civilization uncertain, must know the *Communist Manifesto*.

Among the Great Books, this is a surprisingly short one. It contains only 15,000 words, about 3,000 of which are devoted to a rather dull survey of the socialist literature and the political situation at the time of its writing. In later years, when new editions were prepared, the authors pondered whether they should drop or rewrite that portion. They decided they should not, since the *Communist Manifesto* had become an historical document. Only a few footnotes and a new Preface were added by one of the co-authors, Friedrich Engels, who survived his friend Karl Marx by many years.

Except for the few passages just mentioned, the *Communist Manifesto* is one of the most forceful works of propaganda ever composed by man. Written and published in the midst of the social and political turmoil which immediately preceded the revolutions of 1848 in France, Prussia, Austria, Hungary and Italy, the work reveals the goals of every social revolution to come in our day. The traditionalists, say the authors of the Manifesto, accuse them of the intention to abolish property, freedom, the family, the fatherland, the traditional culture. Yes, they continue, they really have these intentions. But in planning their revolution they merely want to legalize and make universal the trends which, in embryo, already prevail in bourgeois society (the term they use to designate the social system known today as the system of free enterprise). They want to abolish private property; the bourgeois have already abolished it for nine-tenths of the population. They want to abolish freedom in its bourgeois meaning— the freedom to buy and sell everything, including human labor. They want to abolish the traditional family; but there is no need to inaugurate the communization of women since it has existed since time immemorial and, in bourgeois society, means that bourgeois men have at their disposal the wives and daughters of the proletarians. They want to abolish the individual nations; the proletarian has no fatherland. They want to abolish the existing culture, for the ruling ideas of every epoch are the ideas of the ruling class and, with the passing of private property as a means of production, the ideas generated by the bourgeois must and will go.

The authors of the Manifesto recognized that their program was not new: others had already preached socialization of the means of production, the abolition of the traditional family, and so on. But, they asserted, for the first time in history a group of men were basing the order of the future not on dreams or speculation, but on the study of actual relations between men in the past and present. This order, they claim, is not a mere plan, but a scientific prediction. It will be realized, because the Communists expound the program of the proletariat, and the victory of the latter is inevitable. Why? Because in the midst of bourgeois society the proletariat is the only revolutionary class and, throughout history, the class representing a new order of production and exchange has always defeated the class representing an obsolescent order.

Moreover, the Manifesto ascribed to the proletariat the providential role of terminating one of the greatest social evils, the class structure of society and the exploitation of men by men. Class struggle, said Marx and Engels, has always been the general law of history. Through class struggle humanity had advanced from the ancient slave-holding society to feudal society and from feudal society to bourgeois society; and it will advance from bourgeois society to communist society.

In the earlier stages of development, says the Manifesto, the revolutionary class had its particular selfish interests, since it always owned something; therefore, revolutionaries carried out their revolutions in their own interests. The bourgeoisie has, however, accomplished something unprecedented; it has deprived the proletariat of everything except manual strength. The bourgeois pays the laborers just subsistence wages, enough for bare survival and reproduction. It cannot do otherwise because labor forms part of the means of production. In consequence, gaining victory, the proletariat cannot use it in its own special interest. It will gain victory for all men and create a classless society.

Ascribing to the proletariat this providential role was a masterpiece of propaganda. You can incite man to act by showing him that a certain action well serves his interest, but you can treble the force of his zeal by showing him that, acting in his interest, he also takes care of the common good. Add to this the certainty of victory and the allegedly scientific—i.e. irrefutable—character of the reasoning, and you will understand the impact of the Manifesto on many members of the class to which it was addressed and on intellectuals aware of the many injustices and irrationalities of the social order around them.

In their later works, Marx and Engels lent much more precision and allegedly scientific background to the statements of the *Communist Manifesto*. But never did they again expound their views with the same force. Two examples will suffice.

A careful and well-trained reader can find in the Manifesto the hypothesis—later explicitly formulated by Marx in his *Critique of Political Economy*—that the social relations of production evolve independently of human will and, evolving, unilaterally determine all other phases of human co-existence, such as religion, morals, philosophy, art, literature, not to speak of political organization. But, in the Manifesto, the hypothesis is veiled and, in consequence, not exposed to obvious objections.

Moreover, one can find in the Manifesto the dialectical scheme of Marxism, the assertion that everything—including the social relations of production—develops according to the Hegelian triad: in other words, everything passes through the phases of thesis, antithesis and synthesis. The cumbersome efforts made in the authors' later works to explain the history of mankind in terms of these triads make them exceedingly dull reading. In the Manifesto, the idea is present, but appears in concrete and readable form.

The *Communist Manifesto* is a great book because it proved forceful enough to convert millions of minds. But it is also a vicious book because it converts men to fallacy. Therefore one should know its basic weaknesses. By pointing them out, one is able to combat its appeal to those who do not see that the teaching of the Manifesto is a system of ideas incompatible with the principles of Christianity and sound philosophy. Those who reject it on these grounds do not need any refutation.

Here are some points to be made in demonstrating the fallacy of the Manifesto to those who are on the verge of being persuaded. First, its scientific character is asserted, but is conspicuous by its absence. The reasoning is of the type which prevailed in the day of Marx and Engels and continued often to be used, up to the end of the nineteenth century. It consists of an almost childish simplification and schematization of the enormously complicated social phenomena. The Manifesto is right when it asserts that, throughout history, there has been class struggle; but there is no valid reason for its declaration that class struggle is the cause, the only cause, of everything that happens in human society. It ignores the fact that, in addition to antagonism, there is, among men, evidence of much solidarity and cooperation; and that, throughout history, antagonisms between individuals and between social groups have been provoked not only by conflicting economic interests, but also by religious dissent and by emotions based on what we today call exaggerated nationalism.

Only by distorting facts and making bold and unsupported assertions are the authors of the Manifesto able to insist on the paramount importance of the economic factor as expressed in the class struggle.

Second, in analyzing what they call bourgeois society, the authors take it for granted that, in that society, labor can receive only subsistence wages. Such was approximately the situation when they wrote their book; and their charge was based on facts which Engels had previously published in a remarkable book on the state of the laboring class in England. Today, a century after the publication of the Manifesto, one knows their assertion that bourgeois society cannot do otherwise was wrong. He who would today write a book on the state of the laboring class in the United

States and in the advanced countries of Western Europe (prior to the second World War) could not but report an almost miraculous rise in the standards of living of the laborers. The bourgeois order is able to grant to labor a considerable participation in material achievements and in culture. Therefore, it is not necessarily doomed, as was asserted by the authors of the Manifesto.

Third, a strong argument against the Manifesto may be drawn from events in Russia. There, the communist revolution represented largely the application of the principles of the Manifesto; but today, thirty years after, there is little doubt that the division of men into social classes has re-appeared. The top group consists of leaders of the political machine and the economic system; a second group is composed of fellow travelers among the authors, artists, etc.; a third group is the residue. The interests of the groups are conspicuously opposed to one another, and the new ruling class misses no opportunity to consolidate its privileges and transmit them to its progeny. It seems that, to make a human aggregation a going concern, a certain differentiation between organizers and passive participants in an organized effort is necessary, and that this differentiation must be further augmented by higher awards to the members of the active group than to those of the other. This is completely at variance with the teaching of the Manifesto which, in consequence, would incite men to undertake an impossible revolution and to abolish the very condition of social efficiency.

Concluding, one can say that the *Communist Manifesto* aims at impossible goals. Its pretensions to being scientific are utterly false. Its effect has been to unite into a mighty world union all the forces of evil. The fate of humanity depends on the ability of Christians to demonstrate, by words and deeds, the fallacy of this "great book."

NICHOLAS S. TIMASHEFF

SELECTED BIBLIOGRAPHY

GURIAN, Waldemar, *Bolshevism: Theory and Practice*. Sheed and Ward.
HOOK, Sidney, *Toward the Understanding of Karl Marx*. Day.
SCHWARZSCHILD, L., *The Red Prussian*. Scribners.
TIMASHEFF, N. S., *The Great Retreat*. Dutton.
EBON, M., *World Communism Today*. Whittlesey House.
MARX, Karl, *The Communist Manifesto*. Random (Modern Library).

The Bible: Selections

FOR THE Old Testament, Catholics accept Wisdom, Ecclesiasticus, Baruch, First and Second Machabees as part of the canonical scriptures. Also, following the Septuagint (the translation of the Old Testament into Greek between 300 and 130 B.C.), Catholics include some passages in Esther and Daniel rejected by large bodies of Protestants. Those who hold that these writings are not inspired call them "apocryphal." Catholics restrict the term "apocryphal" to other writings, as the Prayer of Manasses, about whose inspiration there was at one time some doubt, but which were finally rejected by all.

The books of the Old Testament accepted as canonical by both Protestants and Catholics are sometimes named differently by the respective groups. Thus what Protestants call I and II Samuel, Catholics call I and II Kings, while the Protestant I and II Kings are for Catholics III and IV Kings. Proper names in the Catholic version are sometimes transliterated differently by Catholics from the spelling used by Protestants. For example, what Protestants call Ezra, Catholics call Esdras, Uriah becomes Urias, etc.

The numbering of the Psalms in Protestant and Catholic versions differs, because Protestants divide Psalm X into two Psalms, making Psalm X and Psalm XI. The Catholic Psalm XI is therefore Psalm XII for Protestants, and so on. But the same Psalms (though numbered differently) are accepted by Catholics and Protestants as inspired, and both reject Psalm 151. Again, the numbering of the Ten Commandments differs between Catholics and Protestants, but both have the same Commandments.

J. ELLIOTT ROSS

II SAMUEL (King James)

Chapter 11

And it came to pass, after the year was expired, at the time when kings go forth to battle, that David sent Joab, and his servants with him, and all Israel; and they destroyed the children of Ammon, and besieged Rabbah. But David tarried still at Jerusalem.

And it came to pass in an eveningtide, that David arose from off his bed, and walked upon the roof of the king's house: and from the roof he saw a woman washing herself; and the woman was very beautiful to look upon.

And David sent and enquired after the woman. And one said, Is not this Bathsheba, the daughter of Eliam, the wife of Uriah the Hittite?

And David sent messengers, and took her; and she came in unto him, and he lay with her; for she was purified from her uncleanness; and she returned unto her house.

And the woman conceived, and sent and told David, and said, I am with child.

And David sent to Joab, saying, Send me Uriah the Hittite. And Joab sent Uriah to David.

And when Uriah was come unto him, David demanded of him how Joab did, and how the people did, and how the war prospered.

And David said to Uriah, Go down to thy house, and wash thy feet. And Uriah departed out of the king's house, and there followed him a mess of meat from the king.

But Uriah slept at the door of the king's house with all the servants of his lord, and went not down to his house.

And when they had told David, saying, Uriah went not down unto his house, David said unto Uriah, Camest thou not from thy journey? why then didst thou not go down unto thine house?

And Uriah said unto David, The ark, and Israel, and Judah, abide in tents; and my lord Joab, and the servants of my lord, are encamped in the open fields; shall I then go into mine house, to eat and to drink, and to lie with my wife? as thou livest, and as thy soul liveth, I will not do this thing.

And David said to Uriah, Tarry here to day also, and to morrow I will let thee depart. So Uriah abode in Jerusalem that day, and the morrow.

And when David had called him, he did eat and drink before him; and he made him drunk: and at even he went out to lie on his bed with the servants of his lord, but went not down to his house.

And it came to pass in the morning, that David wrote a letter to Joab, and sent it by the hand of Uriah.

And he wrote in the letter, saying, Set ye Uriah in the forefront of the hottest battle, and retire ye from him, that he may be smitten, and die.

And it came to pass, when Joab observed the city, that he assigned Uriah unto a place where he knew that valiant men were.

And the men of the city went out, and fought with Joab: and there fell some of the people of the servants of David; and Uriah the Hittite died also.

Then Joab sent and told David all the things concerning the war;

And charged the messenger, saying, When thou hast made an end of telling the matters of the war unto the king,

And if so be that the king's wrath arise, and he say unto thee, Wherefore approached ye so nigh unto the city when ye did fight? knew ye not that they would shoot from the wall?

Who smote Abimelech the son of Jerubbesheth? did not a woman cast a piece of a millstone upon him from the wall, that he died in Thebez? why went ye nigh the wall? then say thou, Thy servant Uriah the Hittite is dead also.

So the messenger went, and came and shewed David all that Joab had sent him for.

And the messenger said unto David, Surely the men prevailed against us, and came out unto us into the field, and we were upon them even unto the entering of the gate.

And the shooters shot from off the wall upon thy servants; and some of the king's servants be dead, and thy servant Uriah the Hittite is dead also.

Then David said unto the messenger, Thus shalt thou say unto Joab, Let not this thing displease thee, for the sword devoureth one as well as another: make thy battle more strong against the city, and overthrow it: and encourage thou him.

And when the wife of Uriah heard that Uriah her husband was dead, she mourned for her husband.

And when the mourning was past, David sent and fetched her to his house, and she became his wife, and bare him a son. But the thing that David had done displeased the LORD.

Chapter 12

And the LORD sent Nathan unto David. And he came unto him, and said unto him, There were two men in one city; the one rich, and the other poor.

The rich man had exceeding many flocks and herds:

But the poor man had nothing, save one little ewe lamb, which he had bought and nourished up: and it grew up together with him, and with his children; it did eat of his own meat, and drank of his own cup, and lay in his bosom, and was unto him as a daughter.

And there came a traveller unto the rich man, and he spared to take of his own flock and of his own herd, to dress for the way-faring man that was come unto him; but took the poor man's lamb, and dressed it for the man that was come to him.

And David's anger was greatly kindled against the man; and he said to Nathan, As the LORD liveth, the man that hath done this thing shall surely die:

And he shall restore the lamb fourfold, because he did this thing, and because he had no pity.

And Nathan said to David, Thou art the man. Thus saith the LORD God of Israel, I anointed thee king over Israel, and I delivered thee out of the hand of Saul;

And I gave thee thy master's house, and thy master's wives into thy bosom, and gave thee the house of Israel and of Judah; and if that had been too little, I would moreover have given unto thee such and such things.

Wherefore hast thou despised the commandment of the LORD, to do evil in his sight? thou hast killed Uriah the Hittite with the sword, and hast taken his wife to be thy wife, and hast slain him with the sword of the children of Ammon.

Now therefore the sword shall never depart from thine house;

because thou hast despised me, and hast taken the wife of Uriah the Hittite to be thy wife.

Thus saith the LORD, Behold, I will raise up evil against thee out of thine own house, and I will take thy wives before thine eyes, and give them unto thy neighbour, and he shall lie with thy wives in the sight of this sun.

For thou didst it secretly: but I will do this thing before all Israel, and before the sun.

And David said unto Nathan, I have sinned against the LORD. And Nathan said unto David, The LORD also hath put away thy sin; thou shalt not die.

Howbeit, because by this deed thou hast given great occasion to the enemies of the LORD to blaspheme, the child also that is born unto thee shall surely die.

And Nathan departed unto his house. And the LORD struck the child that Uriah's wife bare unto David, and it was very sick.

David therefore besought God for the child; and David fasted, and went in, and lay all night upon the earth.

And the elders of his house arose, and went to him, to raise him up from the earth: but he would not, neither did he eat bread with them.

And it came to pass on the seventh day, that the child died. And the servants of David feared to tell him that the child was dead: for they said, Behold, while the child was yet alive, we spake unto him, and he would not hearken unto our voice: how will he then vex himself, if we tell him that the child is dead?

But when David saw that his servants whispered, David perceived that the child was dead: therefore David said unto his servants, Is the child dead? And they said, He is dead.

Then David arose from the earth, and washed, and anointed himself, and changed his apparel, and came into the house of the LORD, and worshipped: then he came to his own house; and when he required, they set bread before him, and he did eat.

Then said his servants unto him, What thing is this that thou hast done? thou didst fast and weep for the child, while it was alive; but when the child was dead, thou didst rise and eat bread.

And he said, While the child was yet alive, I fasted and wept: for I said, who can tell whether God will be gracious to me, that the child may live?

But now he is dead, wherefore should I fast? can I bring him back again? I shall go to him, but he shall not return to me.

And David comforted Bathsheba his wife, and went in unto her, and lay with her: and she bare a son, and he called his name Solomon: and the LORD loved him.

And he sent by the hand of Nathan the prophet; and he called his name Jedidiah, because of the LORD.

And Joab fought against Rabbah of the children of Ammon, and took the royal city.

And Joab sent messengers to David, and said, I have fought against Rabbah, and have taken the city of waters.

Now therefore gather the rest of the people together, and encamp against the city, and take it: lest I take the city, and it be called after my name.

And David gathered all the people together, and went to Rabbah, and fought against it, and took it.

And he took their king's crown from off his head, the weight whereof was a talent of gold with the precious stones: and it was set on David's head. And he brought forth the spoil of the city in great abundance.

And he brought forth the people that were therein, and put them under saws, and under harrows of iron, and under axes of iron, and made them pass through the brickkiln: and thus did he unto all the cities of the children of Ammon. So David and all the people returned unto Jerusalem.

I KINGS (King James)

Chapter 21

And it came to pass after these things, that Naboth the Jezreelite had a vineyard, which was in Jezreel, hard by the palace of Ahab king of Samaria.

And Ahab spake unto Naboth, saying, Give me thy vineyard, that I may have it for a garden of herbs, because it is near unto my house: and I will give thee for it a better vineyard than it; or, if it seem good to thee, I will give thee the worth of it in money.

And Naboth said to Ahab, The LORD forbid it me, that I should give the inheritance of my fathers unto thee.

And Ahab came into his house heavy and displeased because

of the word which Naboth the Jezreelite had spoken to him: for he had said, I will not give thee the inheritance of my fathers. And he laid him down upon his bed, and turned away his face, and would eat no bread.

But Jezebel his wife came to him, and said unto him, Why is thy spirit so sad, that thou eatest no bread?

And he said unto her, Because I spake unto Naboth the Jezreelite, and said unto him, Give me thy vineyard for money; or else, if it please thee, I will give thee another vineyard for it: and he answered, I will not give thee my vineyard.

And Jezebel his wife said unto him, Dost thou now govern the kingdom of Israel? arise, and eat bread, and let thine heart be merry: I will give thee the vineyard of Naboth the Jezreelite.

So she wrote letters in Ahab's name, and sealed them with his seal, and sent the letters unto the elders and to the nobles that were in his city, dwelling with Naboth.

And she wrote in the letters, saying, Proclaim a fast, and set Naboth on high among the people:

And set two men, sons of Belial, before him, to bear witness against him, saying, Thou didst blaspheme God and the king. And then carry him out, and stone him, that he may die.

And the men of his city, even the elders and the nobles who were the inhabitants in his city, did as Jezebel had sent unto them, and as it was written in the letters which she had sent unto them.

They proclaimed a fast, and set Naboth on high among the people.

And there came in two men, children of Belial, and sat before him: and the men of Belial witnessed against him, even against Naboth, in the presence of the people, saying, Naboth did blaspheme God and the king. Then they carried him forth out of the city, and stoned him with stones, that he died.

Then they sent to Jezebel, saying, Naboth is stoned, and is dead.

And it came to pass, when Jezebel heard that Naboth was stoned, and was dead, that Jezebel said to Ahab, Arise, take possession of the vineyard of Naboth the Jezreelite, which he refused to give thee for money: for Naboth is not alive, but dead.

And it came to pass, when Ahab heard that Naboth was dead, that Ahab rose up to go down to the vineyard of Naboth the Jezreelite, to take possession of it.

And the word of the LORD came to Elijah the Tishbite, saying,

Arise, go down to meet Ahab king of Israel, which is in Samaria: behold, he is in the vineyard of Naboth, whither he is gone down to possess it.

And thou shalt speak unto him, saying, Thus saith the LORD, Hast thou killed, and also taken possession? And thou shalt speak unto him, saying, Thus saith the LORD, In the place where dogs licked the blood of Naboth shall dogs lick thy blood, even thine.

And Ahab said to Elijah, Hast thou found me, O mine enemy? And he answered, I have found thee: because thou hast sold thyself to work evil in the sight of the LORD.

Behold, I will bring evil upon thee, and will take away thy posterity, and will cut off from Ahab him that pisseth against the wall, and him that is shut up and left in Israel,

And will make thine house like the house of Jeroboam the son of Nebat, and like the house of Baasha the son of Ahijah, for the provocation wherewith thou hast provoked me to anger, and made Israel to sin.

And of Jezebel also spake the LORD, saying, The dogs shall eat Jezebel by the wall of Jezreel.

Him that dieth of Ahab in the city the dogs shall eat; and him that dieth in the field shall the fowls of the air eat.

But there was none like unto Ahab, which did sell himself to work wickedness in the sight of the LORD, whom Jezebel his wife stirred up.

And he did very abominably in following idols, according to all things as did the Amorites, whom the LORD cast out before the children of Israel.

And it came to pass, when Ahab heard those words, that he rent his clothes, and put sackcloth upon his flesh, and fasted, and lay in sackcloth, and went softly.

And the word of the LORD came to Elijah the Tishbite, saying,

Seest thou how Ahab humbleth himself before me? because he humbleth himself before me, I will not bring the evil in his days: but in his son's days will I bring the evil upon his house.

*   *   *

II Kings (Douay)

Chapter 11

And it came to pass at the return of the year, at the time when kings go forth to war, that David sent Joab and his servants with him, and all Israel, and they spoiled the children of Ammon, and besieged Rabbath: but David remained in Jerusalem.

In the mean time it happened that David arose from his bed after noon, and walked upon the roof of the king's house: and he saw from the roof of his house a woman washing herself, over against him: and the woman was very beautiful.

And the king sent, and inquired who the woman was. And it was told him, that she was Bethsabee the daughter of Eliam, the wife of Urias the Hethite.

And David sent messengers, and took her, and she came in to him, and he slept with her: and presently she was purified from her uncleanness:

And she returned to her house having conceived. And she sent and told David, and said: I have conceived.

And David sent to Joab, saying: Send me Urias the Hethite. And Joab sent Urias to David.

And Urias came to David. And David asked how Joab did, and the people, and how the war was carried on.

And David said to Urias: Go into thy house, and wash thy feet. And Urias went out from the king's house, and there went out after him a mess of meat from the king.

But Urias slept before the gate of the king's house, with the other servants of his lord, and went not down to his own house.

And it was told David by some that said: Urias went not to his house. And David said to Urias: Didst thou not come from thy journey? why didst thou not go down to thy house?

And Urias said to David: The ark of God and Israel and Juda dwell in tents, and my lord Joab and the servants of my lord abide upon the face of the earth: and shall I go into my house, to eat and to drink, and to sleep with my wife? By thy welfare and by the welfare of thy soul I will not do this thing.

Then David said to Urias: Tarry here to day, and to morrow I will send thee away. Urias tarried in Jerusalem that day and the next.

And David called him to eat and to drink before him, and he

made him drunk: and he went out in the evening, and slept on his couch with the servants of his lord, and went not down into his house.

And when the morning was come, David wrote a letter to Joab: and sent it by the hand of Urias,

Writing in the letter: Set ye Urias in the front of the battle, where the fight is strongest: and leave ye him, that he may be wounded and die.

Wherefore as Joab was besieging the city, he put Urias in the place where he knew the bravest men were.

And the men coming out of the city, fought against Joab, and there fell some of the people of the servants of David, and Urias the Hethite was killed also.

Then Joab sent, and told David all things concerning the battle.

And he charged the messenger, saying: When thou hast told all the words of the battle to the king,

If thou see him to be angry, and he shall say: Why did you approach so near to the wall to fight? knew you not that many darts are thrown from above off the wall?

Who killed Abimelech the son of Jerobaal? did not a woman cast a piece of millstone upon him from the wall, and slew him in Thebes? Why did you go near the wall? Thou shalt say: Thy servant Urias the Hethite is also slain.

So the messenger departed, and came and told David all that Joab had commanded him.

And the messenger said to David: The men prevailed against us, and they came out to us into the field: and we vigorously charged and pursued them even to the gate of the city.

And the archers shot their arrows at thy servants from off the wall above: and some of the king's servants are slain, and thy servant Urias the Hethite is also dead.

And David said to the messenger: Thus shalt thou say to Joab: Let not this thing discourage thee: for various is the event of war: and sometimes one, sometimes another is consumed by the sword: encourage thy warriors against the city, and exhort them that thou mayest overthrow it.

And the wife of Urias heard that Urias her husband was dead, and she mourned for him.

And the mourning being over, David sent and brought her into his house, and she became his wife, and she bore him a son: and this thing which David had done, was displeasing to the Lord.

Chapter 12

And the Lord sent Nathan to David: and when he was come to him, he said to him: There were two men in one city, the one rich, and the other poor.

The rich man had exceeding many sheep and oxen.

But the poor man had nothing at all but one little ewe lamb, which he had bought and nourished up, and which had grown up in his house together with his children, eating of his bread, and drinking of his cup, and sleeping in his bosom: and it was unto him as a daughter.

And when a certain stranger was come to the rich man, he spared to take of his own sheep and oxen, to make a feast for that stranger, who was come to him, but took the poor man's ewe, and dressed it for the man that was come to him.

And David's anger being exceedingly kindled against that man, he said to Nathan: As the Lord liveth, the man that hath done this is a child of death.

He shall restore the ewe fourfold, because he did this thing, and had no pity.

And Nathan said to David: Thou art the man. Thus saith the Lord the God of Israel: I anointed thee king over Israel, and I delivered thee from the hand of Saul,

And gave thee thy master's house and thy master's wives into thy bosom, and gave thee the house of Israel and Juda: and if these things be little, I shall add far greater things unto thee.

Why therefore hast thou despised the word of the Lord, to do evil in my sight? Thou hast killed Urias the Hethite with the sword, and hast taken his wife to be thy wife, and hast slain him with the sword of the children of Ammon.

Therefore the sword shall never depart from thy house, because thou hast despised me, and hast taken the wife of Urias the Hethite to be thy wife.

Thus saith the Lord: Behold, I will raise up evil against thee out of thy own house, and I will take thy wives before thy eyes and give them to thy neighbour, and he shall lie with thy wives in the sight of this sun.

For thou didst it secretly: but I will do this thing in the sight of all Israel, and in the sight of the sun.

And David said to Nathan: I have sinned against the Lord. And Nathan said to David: The Lord also hath taken away thy sin: thou shalt not die.

Nevertheless, because thou hast given occasion to the enemies of the Lord to blaspheme, for this thing, the child that is born to thee, shall surely die.

And Nathan returned to his house. The Lord also struck the child which the wife of Urias had borne to David, and his life was despaired of.

And David besought the Lord for the child: and David kept a fast, and going in by himself lay upon the ground.

And the ancients of his house came, to make him rise from the ground: but he would not, neither did he eat meat with them.

And it came to pass on the seventh day that the child died: and the servants of David feared to tell him, that the child was dead. For they said: Behold when the child was yet alive, we spoke to him, and he would not hearken to our voice: how much more will he afflict himself if we tell him that the child is dead?

But when David saw his servants whispering, he understood that the child was dead: and he said to his servants: Is the child dead? They answered him: He is dead.

Then David arose from the ground, and washed and anointed himself: and when he had changed his apparel, he went into the house of the Lord: and worshipped, and then he came into his own house, and he called for bread, and ate.

And his servants said to him: What thing is this that thou hast done? thou didst fast and weep for the child, while it was alive, but when the child was dead, thou didst rise up, and eat bread.

And he said: While the child was yet alive, I fasted and wept for him: for I said: Who knoweth whether the Lord may not give him to me, and the child may live?

But now that he is dead, why should I fast? Shall I be able to bring him back any more? I shall go to him rather: but he shall not return to me.

And David comforted Bethsabee his wife, and went in unto her, and slept with her: and she bore a son, and he called his name Solomon, and the Lord loved him.

And he sent by the hand of Nathan the prophet, and called his name, Amiable to the Lord, because the Lord loved him.

And Joab fought against Rabbath of the children of Ammon, and laid close siege to the royal city.

And Joab sent messengers to David saying: I have fought against Rabbath, and the city of waters is about to be taken.

Now therefore gather thou the rest of the people together, and besiege the city and take it: lest when the city shall be wasted by me, the victory be ascribed to my name.

Then David gathered all the people together, and went out against Rabbath: and after fighting, he took it.

And he took the crown of their king from his head, the weight of which was a talent of gold, set with most precious stones, and it was put upon David's head, and the spoils of the city which were very great he carried away.

And bringing forth the people thereof he sawed them, and drove over them chariots armed with iron: and divided them with knives, and made them pass through brickkilns: so did he to all the cities of the children of Ammon: and David returned, with all the army to Jerusalem.

III KINGS (Douay)

Chapter 21

And after these things, Naboth the Jezrahelite, who was in Jezrahel, had at that time a vineyard near the palace of Achab king of Samaria.

And Achab spoke to Naboth, saying: Give me thy vineyard, that I may make me a garden of herbs, because it is nigh, and adjoining to my house, and I will give thee for it a better vineyard: or if thou think it more convenient for thee, I will give thee the worth of it in money.

Naboth answered him: The Lord be merciful to me, and not let me give thee the inheritance of my fathers.

And Achab came into his house angry and fretting, because of the word that Naboth the Jezrahelite had spoken to him, saying: I will not give thee the inheritance of my fathers. And casting himself upon his bed, he turned away his face to the wall, and would eat no bread.

And Jezabel his wife went in to him, and said to him: What is the matter that thy soul is so grieved? and why eatest thou no bread?

And he answered her: I spoke to Naboth the Jezrahelite, and said to him: Give me thy vineyard, and take money for it: or if it please thee, I will give thee a better vineyard for it. And he said: I will not give thee my vineyard.

Then Jezabel his wife said to him: Thou art of great authority indeed, and governest well the kingdom of Israel. Arise, and eat bread, and be of good cheer, I will give thee the vineyard of Naboth the Jezrahelite.

So she wrote letters in Achab's name, and sealed them with his ring, and sent them to the ancients, and the chief men that were in his city, and that dwelt with Naboth.

And this was the tenor of the letters: Proclaim a fast, and make Naboth sit among the chief of the people,

And suborn two men, sons of Belial against him, and let them bear false witness: that he hath blasphemed God and the king: and then carry him out, and stone him, and so let him die.

And the men of his city, the ancients and nobles, that dwelt with him in the city, did as Jezabel had commanded them, and as it was written in the letters which she had sent to them:

They proclaimed a fast, and made Naboth sit among the chief of the people.

And bringing two men, sons of the devil, they made them sit against him: and they, like men of the devil, bore witness against him before the people, saying: Naboth hath blasphemed God and the king: wherefore they brought him forth without the city, and stoned him to death.

And they sent to Jezabel, saying: Naboth is stoned, and is dead.

And it came to pass when Jezabel heard that Naboth was stoned, and dead, that she said to Achab: Arise and take possession of the vineyard of Naboth the Jezrahelite, who would not agree with thee, and give it thee for money: for Naboth is not alive, but dead.

And when Achab heard this, to wit, that Naboth was dead, he arose, and went down to the vineyard of Naboth the Jezrahelite, to take possession of it.

And the word of the Lord came to Elias the Thesbite, saying: Arise, and go down to meet Achab king of Israel, who is in

Samaria: behold he is going down to the vineyard of Naboth, to take possession of it:

And thou shalt speak to him, saying: Thus saith the Lord: Thou hast slain, moreover also thou hast taken possession. And after these words thou shalt add: Thus saith the Lord: In this place, wherein the dogs have licked the blood of Naboth, they shall lick thy blood also.

And Achab said to Elias: Hast thou found me thy enemy? He said: I have found thee, because thou art sold, to do evil in the sight of the Lord.

Behold I will bring evil upon thee, and I will cut down thy posterity, and I will kill of Achab him that pisseth against the wall, and him that is shut up, and the last in Israel.

And I will make thy house like the house of Jeroboam the son of Nabat, and like the house of Baasa the son of Ahias: for what thou hast done, to provoke me to anger, and for making Israel to sin.

And of Jezabel also the Lord spoke, saying: The dogs shall eat Jezabel in the field of Jezrahel.

If Achab die in the city, the dogs shall eat him: but if he die in the field, the birds of the air shall eat him.

Now there was not such another as Achab, who was sold to do evil in the sight of the Lord: for his wife Jezabel set him on,

And he became abominable, insomuch that he followed the idols which the Amorrhites had made, whom the Lord destroyed before the face of the children of Israel.

And when Achab had heard these words, he rent his garments, and put haircloth upon his flesh, and fasted and slept in sackcloth, and walked with his head cast down.

And the word of the Lord came to Elias the Thesbite, saying:

Hast thou not seen Achab humbled before me? therefore, because he hath humbled himself for my sake, I will not bring the evil in his days, but in his son's days will I bring the evil upon his house.

Notes on the Contributors

REV. WALTER FARRELL, O.P. [1902–   ]

Father Farrell obtained his S.T.Lr. (Lectorate in Theology) at the Dominican House of Studies in Washington, D.C., in 1928. His doctorate in Sacred Theology was granted by the University of Fribourg in 1930, and the degree of Master of Sacred Theology was won at Santa Sabina, Rome, in 1940. Father Farrell contributes frequent articles to *The Thomist,* the *Homiletic and Pastoral Review, Proceedings of the American Catholic Philosophical Association, The Torch,* and is the author of *The Essence of the Natural Law* and *A Companion to the Summa.* He is Professor of Theology, the Regent of Studies in the Province of St. Joseph, and President of the Dominican Pontifical Faculty of Theology.

REV. HAROLD C. GARDINER, S.J. [1904–   ]

A native of Washington, D. C., Father Gardiner entered the Society of Jesus in 1922. After classical studies at St. Andrew-on-Hudson, Poughkeepsie, N. Y., philosophical studies at Woodstock College, Woodstock, Md., a period of teaching the classics and English at Canisius College, Buffalo, N. Y., he returned to Woodstock for theological studies and ordination. A year of ascetical theology in Belgium was succeeded by his entering Downing College, Cambridge University, for postgraduate work in English. The outbreak of the war forced his return to the United States in 1940, but he was able to receive his Ph.D. from Cambridge *in absentia,* in 1941. Since 1940 he has been Literary Editor of *America.* He is also Editorial Chairman of the Catholic Book Club and of the Catholic Children's Book Club. His published work, in addition to articles and reviews in *America* and other periodicals, includes *Mysteries End,* a study of the cessation of the medieval religious stage (Yale University Press, 1945), *Tenets for Readers and Reviewers* (America Press, 1942, 1947). The series of articles on the Great Books comprising this volume appeared originally under his editorship in *America.*

WILLIAM JOSEPH GRACE [1910–   ]

Mr. Grace received his Bachelor's degree from Balliol College, Oxford, in 1933, and his Master's degree in 1937. He has taught and lectured at St. Bonaventure's College, Olean, New York, Fordham University, the Seminary of the Immaculate Conception, Huntington, Long Island, and the College of Notre Dame, Staten Island. He is a contributor to reviews and quarterlies, among them *America, Commonweal, Thought, Sewanee Review,* the *Journal of the History of Ideas.* He at present teaches English at Fordham University's School of Education.

REV. ROBERT C. HARTNETT, S.J. [1904–   ]

A graduate of Loyola University of Chicago, and with an M.A. from St. Louis University, Father Hartnett went to Heythrop College, Oxfordshire, England, to obtain his S.T.L., in 1939. His doctorate in political science was granted by Fordham University in 1946. Until 1948 he was Chairman of the Department of Political Science at the University of Detroit. In December, 1948, he was appointed Editor-in-Chief of *America,* the National Catholic Weekly. He is the author of *Equal Rights for Children* (1947) and co-author of *The Marshall Plan.* He is a contributor to *Wellsprings of the American Spirit* (1948).

REV. GEORGE GILMARY HIGGINS [1916–   ]

Father Higgins received the degree of Bachelor of Sacred Theology from St. Mary's Seminary, Mundelein, in 1940, and his doctorate from Catholic University in 1944. He was appointed a member of the staff of the Department of Social Action, the National Catholic Welfare Conference, in May of 1944. In 1946 he became Assistant Director of the Department. He is a guest lecturer in economics at Catholic University and is a regular columnist of the National Catholic Welfare Conference News Service. He is a frequent contributor of articles on economics and other social topics to magazines. He is a member of the Catholic Association for International Peace.

LOUIS J. A. MERCIER [1880–   ]

Dr. Mercier is an emeritus of Harvard University, where, for thirty-five years, he taught courses in French literature and in education. He is now Professor of Comparative Philosophy and Literature at Georgetown University, and Visiting Professor (summers) at l'Université de Montréal and l'Université Laval at Quebec. His degrees include Litt.D., L.H.D., D.Sc., Ed., Dr. ès Lettres, LL.D. His publications include many articles in Catholic and non-Catholic reviews and professional journals in the United States, Canada and France. He is the author of four French textbooks, of *Our Lady of the Birds,* and of three books on humanism: *Le Meuvement Humaniste aux Etats-Unis,* crowned by the French Academy, *The Challenge of Humanism* and *American Humanism and the New Age.*

JEAN PAUL MISRAHI [1910–   ]

Columbia University granted Dr. Misrahi his A.B. in 1929 and his doctorate in 1933. He has studied at the Universities of Paris and Nancy. He was an instructor in romance languages at Brooklyn College from 1933 to 1938. Since 1938 he has been Professor, Associate Professor and Head of the Department of Romance Languages at Fordham University Graduate School. He is a contributor to *Liturgical Arts, Speculum, The French Review* and other magazines. He is a member of the editorial board of *Thought* and the author of *Le Roman des Sept Sages.*

REV. EDWIN A. QUAIN, S.J. [1906–   ]

Father Quain's college degrees of A.B. and M.A. were obtained at Woodstock College, Maryland. His S.T.L. is from the same institution, in 1937. His doctorate in the classics was granted by Harvard University in 1941. From 1941 to 1945 he was an instructor in the classics in the Fordham University

Graduate School; since 1945 he has been an assistant professor in the same subject. He is Editor of the Fordham University Studies. He is a contributor to *America, Traditio,* the *Classical Bulletin, Thought,* and *Speculum.* He is a collaborator in "The Fathers of the Church in Translation." He is author of "St. Jerome and Humanism" in *A Monument to St. Jerome* (Sheed & Ward, 1948), and of "The Mediaeval *Accessus ad Auctores*," *Traditio* III, 215-264.

RT. REV. MSGR. JOHN K. RYAN [1897-   ]

Monsignor Ryan is a graduate of Holy Cross College, Worcester, Massachusetts, of St. Paul Seminary, St. Paul, Minnesota, of the American College in Rome, where he obtained the degree of Bachelor of Sacred Theology, and of the Catholic University of America, where he won his M.A. in 1931 and his doctorate in 1933. In 1947 he was named a domestic prelate by His Holiness, Pope Pius XII. Since 1931 he has been a member of the Philosophical Faculty of the Catholic University of America and he has also taught at the College of St. Teresa and St. Mary's College in Winona, Minnesota, and at Trinity College in Washington, D.C. Monsignor Ryan has contributed many articles on philosophical subjects to *The New Scholasticism, The Modern Schoolman, America, Thought,* the *Commonweal,* the *Catholic World,* and other magazines. He is the author of *Modern War and Basic Ethics, Basic Principles and Problems of Philosophy, Valor Is Not Suicide* and *The Reputation of St. Thomas Aquinas among English Protestant Thinkers in the Seventeenth Century.* He is co-author of *God and My Heart* and *My Communion,* and has contributed to *Essays in Thomism* and *Essays on Catholic Education in the United States.*

BALDUIN VICTOR SCHWARZ [1902-   ]

Dr. Schwarz' graduate studies were made at the Universities of Heidelberg, Köln and Munich. He received his Doctor's degree from the last named institution. He was for some time an Assistant Professor in the Graduate School at the University of Muenster. He left Germany voluntarily at the rise of Hitler and taught at various universities and colleges in Switzerland, Austria and France. At the fall of France, he was invited to come to this country on a Rockefeller Foundation scholarship. He is at present Professor of Philosophy at Notre Dame College, Staten Island. In addition to contributing frequent articles to scientific journals, he is the author of three books in German: *Psychology of Tears, Error as a Philosophical Problem* and *Perennial Philosophy.*

F. J. SHEED [1897-   ]

Mr. Sheed is a graduate of Sydney University, in arts and law. In 1926 he and his wife, Maisie Ward, opened the London publishing house of Sheed and Ward. The American house was opened in 1933. Mr. Sheed is the author of many books, including *A Map of Life, Communism and Man, Sidelights on the Catholic Revival,* and *Theology and Sanity.* He has translated some dozen works, including *The Confessions of St. Augustine.* In addition to his writing and publishing, Mr. Sheed has been, for over twenty-five years, a speaker of the Westminster Catholic Evidence Guild, whose purpose is to teach Catholic doctrine and explain the Catholic point of view on the street corner. Mr. Sheed is in charge of training the Guild speakers in London and has addressed well over three thousand street-corner and indoor meetings in England and America.

NICHOLAS S. TIMASHEFF [1886–   ]

Dr. Timasheff received his master's degree in 1910 and his LLD in 1914, both from the University of St. Petersburg. In 1916 he became Assistant, and in 1918 Associate, Professor in the Department of Economics of the Polytechnical Institute of St. Petersburg. In 1923 he was appointed Professor at the University of Prague, having left Russia because of political persecution. In 1928 he moved to Paris to become Assistant Editor-in-Chief of a Russian daily paper. At the same time he taught at the Institute of Slavonic Studies, an annex of the Sorbonne, and at the Franco-Russian Institute. In 1936 he was invited by Harvard University to lecture on sociology. He left Harvard in 1940 to become Assistant Professor of Sociology at Fordham University, where he was promoted to the rank of Associate Professor in 1945. Dr. Timasheff has published a volume on *Probation*, in Russian, and, in German, his *Outline of the Constitutional Law of the Soviets*. In 1925, in collaboration with eight scholars, he published a two-volume work entitled *Soviet Law*. This appeared first in Russian and has been translated into German. His American publications include *An Introduction to the Sociology of Law, One Hundred Years of Probation, Religion in Soviet Russia, The Great Retreat: The Growth and Decline of Communism,* and *Three Worlds: Liberal, Communist and Fascist Society.* He has contributed more than eighty articles to scientific journals in Russian, English, French, German and Italian.

DIETRICH VON HILDEBRAND [1890–   ]

Dr. von Hildebrand received his education at the Ludwig Gymnasium, Munich, and the Universities of Munich and Göttingen. He was Assistant Surgeon at the Polyklinik of Munich and lecturer and Professor at the University of Munich. He has taught at Salzburg in Austria and at schools in Italy. He is at present on the Philosophical Faculty at Fordham University. His books are many, but he is perhaps best known for his classic, *In Defense of Purity: The Catholic Ideals of Purity and Virginity.* Among his other works are *Engelbert Dollfuss* (a biography) and *Liturgy and Personality.*